TH

NEW ZEALAND

ARMY

A History from the 1840's to the 1990's

Compiled by
Major G.J. Clayton RNZAEC

First published 1990
ISBN 0-473-01032-1

Book design: Bob Anderson
Typesetting: Wyatt & Wilson Print, Christchurch.
Printed for the Public Relations of the New Zealand Army
by Wyatt & Wilson Print, Christchurch.
Film and Plates: Xenon Graphics Ltd, Christchurch.
Binding: Cartwrights Ltd, Christchurch.

FOREWORD

The New Zealand Army was founded when European settlement first took place in this country. Its spirit was manifest by the banding together of those first settlers to protect their hearths and homes, a spirit which is still the underlying foundation of all defence forces.

From those small bands the Army has progressed to become an organisation small in number but large in professionalism.

Throughout its history it has maintained and developed its links with the community which has ensured its continued support. It has also ensured that its citizens can quickly become soldiers when called upon to defend their homes and freedom.

Researching and writing the history of New Zealand's Army has been an ongoing task since its genesis in the 1830's. Not surprisingly, the body of available published material grows every year. This work is not intended to challenge the findings of works already painstakingly researched. It is designed to provide, in a single volume, a short history of the more important events and times that have had a direct bearing on the New Zealand Army.

Major General
B. Meldrum, OBE,
Chief of General Staff

Wellington
November 1990

ACKNOWLEDGEMENTS

In compiling even a brief history, numerous debts of gratitude are incurred. Major General Meldrum, the Chief of General Staff, by giving his blessing has enabled this work to be produced. Captain Sam Bassett, the Army Public Relations officer, was the instigator of the project, while Lieutenant Barbara Smith, Assistant Public Relations Officer (Army), has brought the publication to completion. The staffs of National Archives, Alexander Turnbull Library, National Museum and the Queen Elizabeth II Army Memorial Museum are to be congratulated on their professionalism as well as assistance. In particular, Elizabeth Cottrell of the Army Museum, who has helped on the research and the typing of this work, deserves special mention.

The largest debt, however, is to the Army and its personnel; they have created an institution that has provided an example of service worthy of emulation.

It only requires to be added, that though many have helped, only the compiler is responsible for any mistakes.

The authors wish to thank the following for permission to use photographic material:

New Zealand Volunteers training — Canterbury Museum, p27.
New Zealand Volunteer Officers training to defend their shore — RNZAF Photographic Section, Waiouru, p37.
Raising the funds and troops to fight — DAC Communicate N.Z., p63.
South Africa: Resting after the long trek — Historical Publications Dept of Internal Affairs, p69.
Departure of New Zealand troops for Europe — N.Z. Herald, p86.
ANZAC Landing — Turnbull Library, p88.
Gallipoli: Charging the Turk — Turnbull Library, p90.
Gallipoli: Advancing on the Enemy — RNZAF Photographic Section, Waiouru, p91.
New Zealanders: Charge forward with fixed bayonets — N.Z. Herald, p92.
Stretcher bearers carry a man out off the Flanders mud — N.Z. Herald, p100.
Crete: German parachute descent — Historical Publications Branch, Dept of Internal Affairs, p117.
Crete: Exhausted New Zealanders in retreat — Turnbull Library, p117.
Tunisia: Signpost on the way to Enfidaville — Turnbull Library, p123.
Tunisia: New Zealand Mule Pack Company — Turnbull Library, p123.
Korea: Kiwi Hill, H.Q. 16th Field Regiment — Turnbull Library, p134.
Korea: The New Zealand Concert Party — Turnbull Library, p135.
Compulsory military training — Elmar Studios, p155.
Training in the 1970's: An integrated Army — DAC Communicate, p158.

CONTENTS

INTRODUCTION

Though the New Zealand Army is less than 150 years old, it has a unique richness of history. From small, ill equipped, badly organised and trained bodies, concerned with protecting little more than isolated hamlets, it has developed into an integrated, professional force of Regular and Territorial units enhancing the stability and security of the South Pacific.

Born from the need to secure personal property, the European Volunteer bands of early nineteenth century New Zealand quickly became recognizable military units. Raised in response to internal threats, they soon laid the foundations of a tradition of valiant and faithful service, foundations that were to be tested and developed at home and on the battlefields of Europe, Africa, Asia and the Pacific.

In more recent times representatives of the New Zealand Army have proved themselves equal to the challenge of peackeeping in the war torn regions of the world. While at Home, and in the Pacific, they provide essential resources for disaster relief, search and rescue and epidemic control. At the same time the Army maintains its readiness for its primary role, national security.

The challenges of war, met with fortitude, have been paralleled by the challenges of peace. New Zealanders have historically been apathetic to the needs of its defence forces, except in time of crises. For over a century and a half, the Army has had to accept reviews, reorganisations, reductions and revivals that would probably have destroyed any other institution.Fluctuating fortunes, in fact have inculcated a flexibility in thought and approach that would be the envy of most business executives. Yet flexibility in itself is insufficient to overcome problems of inadequate resources and training. This is perhaps best shown by the time taken to recoup from the drastic cuts of the depression to meet the threat of European fascism.

In any future conflict the Army will probably not have the luxury of time to prepare. One only has to look at the recent events in the Middle East to realise this. New Zealanders today would be well advised to recall the words of Plato: "Nothing can be more important than that the work of a soldier should be well done. No tools will make a man a skilled workman or master of defence, nor be of any use to him who has not learned how to handle them and has never bestowed any attention upon them."

Chapter One:
ORIGINS

Officially born on the 25 March 1845 with the signing of the country's first Militia Ordinance into law, New Zealand's Army had its origins a decade earlier. The first European New Zealand military force was an embryonic volunteer unit, the Kororareka Association. Formed in 1834, the association had an intermittent existence until 1838. When established, the organisation's task was the preservation of the persons and property of Kororareka. Each member of the Association was required to arm himself with a musket, bayonet, brace of pistols, a cutlass and thirty rounds of ball cartridge.

Equally as important as the Kororareka Association, was the New Zealand Company Militia. In September 1839 at Gravesend, just as the first New Zealand Company emigrant ships were about to set sail, G. F. Young a director of the company held a series of meetings to gain support for the establishment of a defence force. The majority of the emigrants were convinced by Young's arguments of the necessity of an armed force to preserve both peace and property and quickly signed up for the Voluntary Militia. The emigrants agreed that males from 18 to 60 years of age would muster for drill under the command of the company's principal agent for one hour each week. The company, on the other hand, accepted the responsibility of arming the militia as well as organising the training programme. With the signing of the Treaty of Waitangi on 6 February 1840, and formal annexation of New Zealand by Britain, central authority was exercised by the office of Governor. One of the many problems faced by Hobson, the first Governor, was maintenance of security. Lamenting that no adequate provision had been made for a defence force for the new colony, Hobson was advised to make his own arrangements for raising a militia or armed constabulary. While it would appear that the logical course of action would have been to develop the existing forces, Hobson was apprehensive that, as basically private armies, they would not carry out the directives of the central authorities. His concern was so great that he outlawed the New Zealand Company Volunteer Militia. Unfortunately he did not replace the colonists' self-help measure for defence with any other structure. The result of this neglect was, that when trouble threatened in 1841 settlers readily reformed their voluntary armed bands. At Kororareka, Auckland and Wanganui 'volunteer' units sprang up and were quickly organized into squads and commenced formal training programmes under ex-regular soldiers.

There was a similar result in June 1843 at Nelson in response to the Wairau Affray. Twenty-two surveyors and settlers were killed when they attempted to arrest Te Rauparaha and Te Rangihaeata. When news of the fight reached Nelson, panic swept through the settlement. Fearing a Maori assault on the town, agitated settlers commenced organizing their defences. A central defence organizing committee of leading citizens was immediately appointed to take charge. A volunteer force was embodied, arms and ammunition from the New Zealand company warehouse issued, a training programme devised and a redoubt constructed. Across Cook Strait, in Nelson's sister New Zealand Company settlement Wellington, a similar response was given when the same alarm gripped the colonists. A 400 strong Volunteer Militia was formed that met daily for training, redoubts were built and gun positions constructed.

Active measures for defence by the Cook Strait settlements, was in marked contrast to the inactivity of the Governor. Fitzroy, believing the Nelson settlers were in the wrong over Wairau, refused to take any action against either Te Rauparaha or Te Rangihaeata. This course of action, or more correctly inaction, resulted in a waning of European anxiety as the Ngati Toa responded in a like manner. This waning was, however, to be relatively short lived. Within a year the seeds were to be sown for the outbreak of hostilities that spread throughout the northern half of the colony. From Kororareka to Nelson, settlers troubled by the turbulence again looked to their defences and again voluntarily banded together for mutual protection. The seeds sown on 8 July 1844 were the result of the the Ngapuhi followers of Hone Heke Pokai cutting down the flagstaff at Kororareka. This symbol of British authority was felled by Heke, who was convinced that it challenged the mana of the chiefs. Fearing for their safety, the European inhabitants of Kororareka prepared for war. To avoid a collision, another prominent Ngapuhi chief, Tamati Waka Nene, calmed Heke and convinced him to replace the fallen flagstaff. For six months Nene's negotiated calm prevailed until Heke's followers again brought down the flagstaff on 10 January 1845. Incensed by this second outrage Fitzroy was goaded into activity. He offered a reward for the capture of Hone Heke, sent for troop reinforcements from New South Wales and ordered the re-erection of the flagstaff. In response Heke contemptuously had the symbolic stick of British authority felled for the third time on 19 January 1845. Determined not to be got the best of, Fitzroy ordered Kororareka to be put on virtually a war footing. The flagstaff was once more erected, this time sheathed with iron, while around the town and flagstaff, blockhouses, earthworks and gun positions were constructed. In addition, a Kororareka Volunteer unit, the 'civil guard', was raised and trained to supplement the troops.Unfortunately these preparations were unco-ordinated due to the lack of an overall commander. The result was formidable defence works that existed in splendid isolation, unable to support each other. This lack of mutual support was fully exploited by the assault forces of Heke and Kawiti on 11 March 1845. They not only toppled the flagstaff, but also the town, leaving it a smoking ruin and killing 13 settlers.

When news of the sacking of Kororareka reached the capital, Auckland, panic reigned. Fearing a direct assault on Auckland, large numbers took the first ship out. Those left behind followed the now well practised pattern of reviewing their defences. Immediately to strengthen those defences a Volunteer company was embodied. Unlike previous panics which tended to be very localised affairs, the anxiety caused by the fall of Kororareka spread throughout the colony. In Taranaki, Wanganui, Wellington and Nelson, settlers believed emboldened Maoris were preparing to challenge British authority. Community leaders quickly channeled the unproductive anxiety into enthusiastic support for local defence initiatives. In Wellington, for example, the resident Magistrates organised the construction of fortifications, places of refuge, the raising of a volunteer corps and the appointment of officers, the distribution of training manuals, the provision of drill sergeants, the production of a training timetable, alarm procedures, patrols, pickets, and the distribution of arms, ammunition and equipment. Similar provisions were made by all settlements anxious lest they be attacked.

It is somewhat surprising, given the disturbed state of the colony, that the Governor did not arrange for the formation of a military force. After all local responses tended to arise from an immediate panic rather than from careful consideration of need. In fact, Fitzroy had toyed with the idea of establishing a standardised Militia force, but was reluctant lest the settlers once armed and trained provoke rather than prevent hostilities. When settlers once again took matters into their own hands and commenced their own ad hoc and disjointed defensive preparations, Fitzroy was forced to act. On 25 March 1845 he arranged for the first New Zealand Militia ordinance to be passed by the Legislative Council. This ordinance provided a standardised infrastructure for the raising of citizen forces. Males between the ages of 18 and 60 were liable for military service within a 25 mile radius of their nearest police office. Authority was vested firmly in central government and one of the Government's first actions under the ordinance, was to force the disbandment of the various volunteer companies that individual settlements had raised.These companies were immediately replaced by units of the new Militia. Defence had finally become a central government concern, too important to be left solely to well meaning but not necessarily well considered local initiatives.

Chapter Two:

THE NEW ZEALAND WARS 1845-72

While Fitzroy's staff worked on ways of providing an infrastructure for the command and control of localised defence measures forty five volunteers from the Auckland Militia joined the hastily organised expedition north. In the campaigns against Heke and Kawiti, these volunteers acted as assault pioneers, porters carrying forward the hospital establishment, as artillerymen manning the ships guns brought ashore to provide additional firepower to the assaulting forces, as engineers constructing roads and stockades and as guides to the Imperial forces. Further south, in Wellington, other volunteers also undertook active service with the Imperial forces, assisting in several skirmishing operations in the Lower Hutt area as well as serving as garrison troops manning redoubts and conducting patrols. The efficiency and effectiveness of the volunteers on active service in the 1840's not only won praise, it also proved that the settlers' willingness to band together for protection was matched by sufficient military skill to provide that protection. It also provided an embryonic model for working relationships between the Imperial Army and locally raised citizen forces.

The working relationships between the forces of the Empire and colony were significantly enhanced by the number of ex-regular servicemen who made their home in New Zealand. Of New Zealand's total male population of nearly 34,000 in 1858 over 2,000, or approximately six percent, are readily identifiable as ex-regular force servicemen. This six percent was constituted from three basic categories. The first category was those soldiers stationed in New Zealand and who had requested their discharge in the colony. The second group was those soldiers discharged elsewhere who had subsequently made their own way to the colony. By far the largest group of ex-regulars, were those who requested their discharge in New Zealand. One Regiment, the 58th, had over one thousand of its members take their discharge in New Zealand between 1845 and 1858. More difficult to determine, as far as numbers are concerned, are pensioners who made their own way to New Zealand. It is believed, for example, that a large number of the twelve hundred who had travelled to Australia between 1849 and 1850 came to New Zealand, but exact figures are unavailable. The last group were the fencibles who were assisted to migrate between 1847 to 1852. Recruited in the United Kingdom the 'Royal New Zealand Fencibles' numbered just over seven hundred.

Brought out at the conclusion of the Northern War, the Fencibles were designed to act as a cordon sanitaire for the capital. Interestingly, they were settled on the southern approach routes to the capital. Clearly, at the conclusion of the Northern War the Ngapuhi were no longer seen as a threat, whereas the the tribes of the Waikato Federation were. To protect Auckland's southern frontier the Governor settled the Fencibles, who were to act as sedentary part-time soldiers. The cost to the colony was free passage to New Zealand for the Fencibles and their family, a cottage complete with an acre of land, a regulation uniform, 1/3d per day. For the fencibles the cost was seven years return of service, during which time they were required to muster every Sunday, attend twelve days training each year, work no more than five miles from home and be prepared for immediate mobilisation for active service. However, in its entire existence the Royal New Zealand Fencibles was only once mobilised for service. On the 17th April 1851 they were mobilised to secure vital communication routes and provide an expeditionary force against a two hundred and fifty strong taua (war party) of Ngati Paoa. The taua had been despatched to exact utu (revenge) from a Maori constable who had struck Te Hoera, a Ngati Paoa chief, on the head during a fracas. Fortunately the good offices of the Ngati Whatua defused the situation and calm was quickly restored.

Despite their lack of use, Auckland's Fencibles were coveted by New Zealand's other settlements. In Taranaki, settlers convinced of the military benefits of the fencibles, met to demand similar schemes for their own province. On the opposite coast the local government undertook its own pensioner settlement scheme in 1859. Worried over the escalation of inter tribal fighting during 1858 and 1859, East Coast officials established the equivalent of a fencible settlement at Ormond. Though in the short term they were unused, in the long term, the fencibles proved immensely important. Their training programmes, consisting of weekly meetings and week long encampments, provided a role model for future forces. Further, on completion of their seven years return of service the fencibles were to provide key personnel for subsequently raised defence forces.

Theoretically all fencibles, along with the bulk of the male population, were immediately members of the Militia on completion of their seven year service obligation. In practice, the New Zealand Militia, after 1847, was simply a paper force. When trouble erupted between land sellers and anti-sellers in Taranaki in 1855, the Governor in Council decreed that any Maoris fighting on European land would be treated as rebels. To ensure that sufficient force was available to carry out the edict, Militia enrolment and training was ordered for Auckland, New Plymouth and Wellington.

With the rejuvenation of New Zealand's militia came the realisation that the 1845 Militia Ordinance was inadequate. The hostilities in Taranaki highlighted the inflexibility of New Zealand's defence statute, a statute that did not allow for partial mobilization, or the enrolment of voluntary units or exemptions from service. Recognising the need for change, the newly established government, meeting in Assembly in its first full session in April 1858, agreed to the introduction of a new Militia Bill. Influenced by politics, culture and geography, New Zealand's political leaders refashioned the 1845 Ordinance into an Act more suited to the times. The 1858 Militia Act, which became law in mid-May, restated the pre-eminent position of the compulsory Militia while at the same time allowing for the establishment of voluntary units.

Within two years of its passage, the 1858 Act was to be tested by the resumption of hostilities within New Zealand. Governor Gore Browne's determination to proceed with the purchase of the 600 acre Pekupeku block at Waitara, led to the fateful break with Wiremu Kingi. Kingi had highlighted his opposition to the proposed sale of his ancestral home by Te Teira but the Governor underestimated his resolve. He assumed that European might would force Kingi to acquiesce. He had not foreseen the resumption of the New Zealand Wars, nor had he foreseen the spread of the conflict over most of the North Island.

The Governor's inability to predict the outcome of his actions is not surprising, given that Colonel Gold, the Commander of the Imperial troops stationed in New Zealand, thought that one volley would be sufficient to subdue the anti-land selling Maori. Acting on this advice the Executive Council decided on 25 January 1860 to proceed with the Waitara purchase and survey the land. If any resistance were to be offered to the survey, martial law was to be proclaimed and the land was to be held by force if necessary. Acting on these instructions, Octavius Carrington attempted to survey the Waitara block on 20 February 1860. The survey was obstructed immediately by Wiremu Kingi's followers. In response Lieutenant-Colonel G. F. Murray, the local commander, declared martial law and called out the Militia and Volunteers for active service. Excited and enthusiastic about the possibility of demonstrating their martial prowess, the response to the government's encouragement was immediate. So many citizens came forward that there were initially insufficient arms to equip them all. Many believed that it was time that the independently-minded Maori be brought to heel by a 'good-licking' from the barrels of massed muskets.

Active service and the threat of hostilities escalating resulted in a massive increase in interest and participation in New Zealand defence forces. In Taranaki, Nelson, Wellington, Wanganui and Auckland new corps were formed at a frantic rate. Immediately they were formed, many units found themselves on duty. In Wellington, for example, dozens of men rushed to join the Rifle Volunteers on the outbreak of war and no sooner had they donned their uniforms, when they were called out for service. They took over the garrison duties at Mount Cook so that the regular force detachment could be freed for service in Taranaki.

The quick growth of units made the government realise that volunteering was becoming extremely popular. As a result, the ministry reviewed the service conditions of the Volunteers and allowed them to serve as independent bodies rather than as junior partners of a Militia-Volunteer combination, as originally conceived in the framing of the 1858 Militia Act. At the same time the Government took the opportunity to re-examine the whole 1858 defence framework in the light of its operational use. To reduce costs and improve on the earlier measure, the 1860 Militia Act Amendment Bill was passed, modelled principally on the Militia acts of Nova Scotia and New Brunswick, the age of those liable for service was reduced from 60 to 55. It also placed the onus on those eligible for service to ensure that their names appeared on the Militia roll. Volunteer units were to be raised in their own right, rather than as part of the Militia.

The encouragement given to New Zealand volunteering proved extremely successful. In 1860, thirty-two new volunteer units were formed. The growth of interest in volunteering resulting from the war and the government's encouragement was in fact so rapid and overwhelming, that the defence authorities were forced to provide an ad hoc general set of regulations outlining the terms which volunteer units would be expected to adhere to. This eight paragraphed set of regulations, gazetted in March 1860, required all volunteers to be available for 168 hours of training per year. The government undertook to supply all basic equipment except uniforms which were to be selected and supplied by the members of the individual corps. In addition to the equipment, the government also undertook to provide a regular force cadre for each militia district. Consisting of an Adjutant and Sergeant-Major this cadre was ultimately respon–

sible for training and examining volunteers, as well as being responsible for communicating with the higher authorities.

Regulatory changes and organisational reforms and examinations, while important for force structure and control, did little to affect the roles assigned to New Zealand's military force. In Taranaki they continued to supply reinforcement for search and destroy operations, reconnaissance and general garrison duties, though after a year of war their enthusiasm had waned. On the eve of the Battle of Matarikoriko only half of the Taranaki citizen soldiers mustered, this so enraged the commander of the force, Lieutenant Colonel Carey, that he ordered their dismissal and replaced them with a detachment from the 12th Regiment. This decline in enthusiasm was probably an outward manifestation of a weariness of a war that had no quick or easy victory. All had had enough and were prepared to accept some form of negotiated peace. General Pratt meanwhile was methodically reducing pas by the time consuming unglamorous sap. Not surprisingly articles of peace were accepted by both sides after the Te Arai Pa surrendered. Though accepted, not all considered them binding. Local papers complained that after fifteen months of strife, turmoil and anxiety Taranaki was still in the same perplexed turbulent state as when hostilities commenced. They predicted that the peace, in fact, was little more than a truce and further hostilities would eventuate.

Media belief that hostilities would be renewed was further fueled by the Governor's determination to strike a decisive blow against the Maori insurgents. On the advice of his Attorney-General, Whitaker, the Governor forwarded to the Kingites an ultimatum demanding that they acquiesce to the new order. The Kingites refused and Browne was forced to contemplate invading the Waikato. The Imperial authorities were dissatisfied with Browne's blundering escalation of hostilities and before he could implement any plans for an invasion of the Waikato he was replaced by Sir George Grey. Immediately on arrival Grey countermanded Browne's orders and endeavoured to reconcile the Kingites to British sovereignty by diplomacy. Grey's policy of conciliation was pursued for eighteen months. Though conciliatory, Grey also prepared for the possibility of war. He organised the reinforcement of the regular force garrisons, arranged for the construction of a military transport road, established a Commissariat Transport Corps and supported the construction of river gunboats in New South Wales shipyards.

A major element in Governor Grey's military build-up was the colony's citizen forces. They undertook the garrison duties for Auckland while the regular force detachments were busy constructing the military road south. More importantly, the citizen forces were again completely restructured. Prior to 1862 the defence authorities in large measure responded to the demands of the citizens. Grey altered this emphasis by instigating yet another examination of the nation's defence requirements and then overhauled the citizen forces. He initiated the passage of the Colonial Defence Act of 1862. This raised the first Regular Force in New Zealand, the Colonial Defence Force, a body of mounted men not to exceed 500 in total. He also encouraged the formation of volunteer units that met direct defence requirements. In January 1862 a new set of volunteer regulations consisting of sixteen paragraphs were drafted, agreed to by the Governor in council and subsequently gazetted. The most important provisions of the new regulations was the total disbandment of the existing volunteer force and the encouragement of individuals to enlist.

More important than the regulations encouraging individuals to join units or the control mechanisms of those units, was the decisions on the total force structure. After careful consultation with General Cameron, the Governor and his council promulgated an establishment for the volunteer force. The colony was divided into nine districts with a detailed list of 33 units eligible for enrollment in each.

Grey also arranged for the enrollment of 'regular Volunteer companies'. Unlike units of the Volunteer force proper, which were enrolled under the provisions of the 1858 Militia Act and its amendments, the 'regular' units were raised under exclusive regulations. Hostilities were renewed in Taranaki when Governor Grey, deciding the Waitara purchase illegal, decided to return it to Kingi. Prior to formally handing back the land, Grey ordered the reoccupation of the Tataraimaka block in Taranaki. Con–

sidering these acts as provocative the Kingites responded by ambushing two escorts and Taranaki was once again transformed from a garden province to a battlefield. Immediately the Taranaki citizen soldiers were to the fore. Determined to take the initiative they formed a Bush Ranger unit under Major H. Atkinson to undertake an aggressive patrolling in the heavily forested lands. Undoubtedly the resumption of war was as important to the expansion of the colony's military forces as was Grey's administrative and organisational reforms. The resumption of war in Taranaki was quickly followed by war in the Waikato. After Cameron crossed the Mangatawhiri, in July 1863, war with the Waikato tribes was inevitable. The commencement of an escalation in hostilities raised fears of attack throughout the North Island, especially when it was realised that the interior tribes had, in fact, amassed a large stockpile of arms and ammunition. The fear of native attack was heightened after the Europeans' destruction of their settlement, while lower down the North Island Wellington settlers feared that there was little hope if the capital could not protect itself.

Cameron's invasion forces pushed forward into the Waikato, forcing the Waikato tribes to retire into the King Country and allowing the vacated lands to be confiscated. To provide long term protection to this new and exposed frontier, the government arranged for the settling of sedentary soldiers, in much the same fashion as the original Fencibles. Four regiments of Waikato Militia were raised and the newly recruited settler-soldiers were offered a farm and rations in return for military service. The government also approved the formation of the 'Forest Rangers' under Major W. Jackson. Based on the Taranaki Bush Rangers, they proved so successful as guerilla fighters that a second company under Major G. F. Von Tempsky was raised.

By 1864 the War in the North Island appeared to be winding down. Rewi Maniapoto had been forced to retreat into the King Country while in the Bay of Plenty the repulse at Gate Pa had been avenged by the slaughter at Te Ranga. However, the de-escalation of the war was not to result in a total cessation of hostilities. Rather it led to a period of transformation from conventional warfare to guerilla, almost terrorist, campaigns. This

March on the beach: Wanganui/Taranaki units.

Picket at 1895 Nuahaka Camp.

new phase in the conflict was ushered in by the rise of the Pai Marire (Good and Peaceful) religion, more commonly referred to as Hau Hau, under the leadership of the prophet Te Ua Haumene. It reached its height under two successful guerilla-terrorist leaders Te Kooti and Titokowaru on the East and West Coasts of the North Island. At the same time that the nature of the New Zealand hostilities was transforming, the responsibility for internal defence of the colony was also changing. Until 1865 the Governor, as Commander-in-chief, had theoretical control over the military, though in practice he delegated his responsibility to the commander of the British Forces. In 1865 significant changes were to occur as a result of the pressure put on the New Zealand colonial government by the Imperial authorities who were determined to reduce the cost of defending the Empire.

The desire of the Imperial Authorities to reduce spending on defence was not new. As early as 1846, Earl Grey had advocated a reduction in Imperial garrisons and the introduction of colonial contributions for local defence. This concept of reduced central spending and increased colonial contribution was more fully developed thirteen years later. An inter-departmental inquiry comprising of representatives from the War Office, Treasury and Colonial Office recommended in 1859, that colonies should make greater efforts in local defence. These calls were followed up in 1861 by a parliamentary select committee under the chairmanship of Arthur Mills. The select committee's report proposed that only strategically important military posts should be manned by Imperial garrisons. All other posts in the Empire, including Canada and the Australasian colonies to be self-reliant. By March 1862 most of Britain's leading politicians accepted the new divisions of responsibility for defence. In that month a resolution was passed through the House of Commons recognising Imperial responsibility for defence against perils arising from Imperial policy but noting that self-governing colonies ought to accept responsibility for internal order, a resolution that was perceived by New Zealand's European colonists as a pointed barb, directed primarily at them. Such a perception had some validity, the Duke of Newcastle, while in charge of the colonial office, believed that the War in New Zealand had been forced

Bluff: Stockade 1862.

upon the Governor by the avaricious colonists. Newcastle's determination was further strengthened by the advice given by J. R. Godley, who argued that colonies should be self-reliant in internal defence for their own benefit and honour.

More importantly, such a scheme was cheaper for the British taxpayer.When Gladstone presented the 1864 budget, it fore–shadowed a reduction in the military vote. This reduction was to be achieved not only be reducing Imperial garrisons but also by a user pays policy for troops. The previous year, self-governing colonies had been informed that for each Imperial soldier stationed on their shores they would be charged £40 per annum. The New Zealand authorities had been closely monitoring the clear signals emanating from London. Indeed, they were constantly endea–

vouring to counter the Imperial Authorities' attempts to force self-reliance for internal defence. At the time of the Mills Select Committee, the New Zealand Parliament formed its own secret bicameral committee to investigate and report on its internal defence requirements. It also reviewed what the colony, should, or should not, pay toward maintaining an Imperial garrison. Given the uncertain state of affairs internally and the size of European population and commerce, the committee hoped that the colony would only have to contribute £5 per soldier. To answer the criticism that the colony had not done sufficient to prepare its citizens for war, the colonial government claimed that they did not wish to project any appearance of aggressive action. Such an appearance, they argued, could be easily misconstrued by the natives and lead to the outbreak of war, which they wished to avoid.

To a large degree, the manoeuvrings by the New Zealand government were a waste of effort. Though the Imperial forces were retained for the large scale invasion operation of the Waikato, the decision to withdraw the garrison remained. By 1870 all Imperial troops were to be recalled from New Zealand. Not all viewed the withdrawal of the Imperial garrison with concern. Some realized self-reliance could be of some benefit as it would end dual control over native affairs. Leading the political initiatives in New Zealand for assuming responsibility of internal defence were William Fox and Frederick Weld. Both were in close communication with Godley, who advised them to take the opportunity to gain control and responsibility for native affairs. Not surprisingly when Weld was called upon to form a ministry in October 1864, he did so on the condition that the self-reliant policy for defence would be supported by the Governor. Within weeks Weld had laid before the House a defence policy for New Zealand in a post-Imperial garrison era. To maintain internal security, Weld proposed a small regular force of 1,500 Armed Constabulary manning frontier positions and supported by citizen soldiers, as and when required.

In 1867 Weld's proposals became firm policy with the passage of the Armed Constabulary Act. Superceeding the 1862 Colonial

New Zealand Volunteers training.

Defence Act, the new Act established a force which consisted of both mounted and infantry units as well as combining military with police functions. At its strongest in the late 1860's, when pursuing Titokowaru and Te Kooti, it numbered nine divisions. Each division had between sixty and eighty constables led by and inspector and controlled by two sub-inspectors assisted by one senior sergeant, three sergeants and three corporals. Aided by Volunteers, Militia and Kupapa (friendly) Maori units, the Armed Constabulary completed the task of subjugating Maori resistance to the authority of the crown. Using a combination of Field Force units together with garrison forces at strategically placed redoubts, the Armed Constabulary proved to be an effective military force. The Field Force undertook search and destroy operations, while the garrisons provided secure bases. In early 1872 they brought the New Zealand Wars to an end, not by formal agreement or treaty, but by the imposition of the reality that armed resistance was no longer viable.

Casualties

During the New Zealand Wars approximately 560 British and Colonial troops were killed whilst on active service and a further 1,050 were wounded. Over the same period approximately 250 Kupapa (friendly) Maori were killed and up to 2,000 "hostile" Maori were killed, with an unknown number of Maori wounded on each side.

New Zealand: 1858 — A Militiaman.

Chapter Three:

FORTRESS NEW ZEALAND

The period from the New Zealand Wars to the South African War can best be described as one of uncertainty. The belief that the native rebellion had been successfully concluded was a minority opinion, as was the view that the international situation was of little importance to New Zealand's security. The majority of colonists held the view that the resumption of the New Zealand Wars was likely. It was also widely believed that New Zealand's shore was extremely vulnerable to foreign aggression. As Major Atkienson so succinctly stated in the House Of Representatives:

> "They did not know when there might be war either internally or externally..."

In retrospect, it is easy to dismiss threats to New Zealand's security in the latter half of the nineteenth century as mere flights of colonial fantasy. Hindsight provides critical commentators with the indisputable knowledge that peace was maintained. It was however, a paranoia based on real concerns not flights of imaginative fantasy. The colonists of New Zealand had, in the 1860's, followed the exploits of the confederate privateers 'Alabama', 'Florida' and 'Shenandoah' with interest. They knew, without doubt, that a solitary vessel designed for speed, that was well armed and fuelled, could easily descend upon their shores, threaten shipping and destroy ports.

New Zealand's awareness of its vulnerability to small-scale raids, was to be a constant concern throughout the century. The governmental response to this concern was a series of defence committees and reviews. On re-examination of the nation's external defence requirements, the committees recommended the installation of heavy gun batteries, complete with an integrated torpedo system. However, little was actually done until the mid 1880's. In part, this was due to cost but it was also due to perceptions of responsibility. New Zealand, as a self-governing colony, had been forced to accept self-reliance for internal security but maintained that Britain should continue to take responsibility for defending the colony from external aggression. It was felt that Britain should bear such responsibility as New Zealand would only face an external aggressor as the result of Britain becoming involved in a war with a European power rather than through any action of its own. If Britain could not defend New Zealand from such aggression, then it was felt, by some at least, that an independent kingdom should be established so that any war involving Great Britain would not automatically involve New Zealand. Most, however, would have preferred to have an independent squadron of the British Navy stationed in the colony to secure its shores.

Britain was, however, unable to guarantee the security of New Zealand's shore from every eventuality. While accepting the responsibility of securing the whole Empire against strategic threat, the British authorities made it abundantly clear that they could not prevent isolated attacks by small, fast, well-armed raiders. British shortcomings in providing total security reinforced the feeling of vulnerability that most New Zealand colonists already had. Coupled with growing tensions amongst the European powers and the extension of their rivalries into the Pacific, New Zealand was gradually forced out of its complacency. France, Germany, the United States as well as the continually growing menace of Russia, loomed as potential aggressors. Russia, with its expansionist policy, its practice of sending its modern naval vessels on long distance training voyages, and its threatening base at Vladivostock became the predominant external threat.

Though none could accurately predict when Britain, and therefore New Zealand, might be involved in war, by early 1878 no one doubted that war with Russia was imminent. The Russian army had advanced on Istanbul; in response the British fleet cleared its decks for action in the sea of Marmora, recruited the Brigade of Guards up to war strength and reinforced both Malta and Gibraltar. Such signals meant only one thing to New Zealand, war between Russia and Britain. Of more immediate concern was the Russian purchase of three merchant ironclads from the United States. The three ships, the State of California, Columbus and Saratoga were refitted and renamed as the Warships Europa (Europe), Asiia (Asia) and Afrika (Africa). In addition, Russia ordered the construction of a fourth ironclad at the Crumps shipyard. When news of these purchases leaked, New York insurance brokers raised premiums for British shipping by a further two percent and the Admiralty ordered its vessels at Bermuda and Halifax to be ready to cruise the North American coasts if required.

In response to the escalation of tensions, the New Zealand Government finally took action for the defence of its shores. It ordered twenty-four artillery pieces at a cost of £44,000. Before these guns arrived, however, the British and Russian tensions were eased by the agreement reached at the Congress of Berlin. With the threat of war receding the New Zealand Government declined to take any further action for its own external defence. British authorities, however, took more positive action by establishing the Colonial Defence committee and setting up a Royal Commission under the chairmanship of Lord Carnarvon. Created to enquire and report on the defences of strategic colonial ports, these bodies undertook the first detailed examination of Imperial defence requirements in the nineteenth century. The commission developed further the concept of colonial self-reliance in defence and noted that, while the Royal Navy was responsible for the protection of British trade on the high seas, protection of colonial harbours was the responsibility of the respective colonial governments.

New Zealand had little choice but to accept these policy guidelines as the government had declined to send a delegation to the commission's hearings even though they had been invited to do so. The cabinet had decided to decline the invitation as they had not formulated a considered policy on coastal defence, a lack they were to overcome by inviting Colonel Scratchley to report on New Zealand's defence needs. In mid-February 1880, Scratchley wrote and presented his recommendations to the New Zealand Government in a 37 page report. To defend New Zealand's coast adequately against likely attacks, Scratchley recommended that fortifications be constructed utilizing the existing heavy artillery pieces and submarine mines. These installations, Scratchley believed, should be manned by a nucleus of regular servicemen supported by a reorganised Volunteer Force. Volunteer units in the immediate hinterland of the principal ports, would be employed either as auxiliaries to the forts, or as members of a Mobile Field Force to counter small scale enemy landings. If a corps could not be employed immediately in the forts or Field Force, Scratchley recommended that they be disestablished. In total, Scratchley believed, only 2,400 of the existing 8,032 Volunteers were required to defend New Zealand's principal ports. To the annoyance of many, the government did not act immediately to implement Scratchley's recommendations. The government was determined to make haste slowly, arguing that Scratchley's report was not complete and they did not wish to take any ill-considered action. Underlying all this hesitancy of the government, was the need to retain the interior corps for use if the Maori insurgents resumed hostilities.

In sharp contrast to the reinforced and highlighted realisation by New Zealand's colonists that their homelands ports and harbours were extremely vulnerable to external attack, was the resurgence of the internal threat. Though the last shots in the New Zealand Wars had been fired in May 1872, colonists were unsure whether they were truly in a state of peace.Maori opposition to surveying and land sales was still widespread and many feared that a resumption of hostilities would occur. Fear of a renewal in hostilities with the Maori was most prevalent in the seats of the last war, Taranaki and Waikato. In Taranaki, for example, Parihaka loomed as a potential centre of rebellion. In the Waikato the southern lands of the Ngati Maniapoto were seen as an asylum,

Fortress New Zealand: Preparing the mines.

Fortress New Zealand: The Garrison Artillery.

not only for the dispossessed and disgruntled Waikato Kingites, but also the fierce guerilla leader Te Kooti. Alarms and war rumours were a frequent occurrence for those living north of the Aukati (confiscation line) which the Kingites enforced as a closed border.This closed border was to be opened when the Waikato threat was finally neutralised through negotiation. Lasting from early 1878 until mid-1881, the negotiations between the Kingites and the government climaxed when King Tawhiao rode into Alexandra on 11 July 1881 at the head of 600 warriors. With his chiefs and his followers, Tawhiao symbolically laid down the weapons of war signifying to all that peace had been finally made.

Tawhiao's reconciliation, while easing tensions on the Waikato frontier, did not dispel the bogey of an internal threat to the colony's security. On the West Coast of the North Island a repeat performance of 1860 seemed to be in the offing with Parihaka taking the place of Waitara. Established on confiscated Taranaki land. Parihaka, by 1879, had become a citadel of Maori nationalist resistance to governmental authority. Under the joint leadership of Te Whiti and Tohu the residents of Parihaka were determined to resist the European settlement of confiscated lands until adequate reserves had been set aside for the original Maori owners. Unlike previous resistance attempts, however, Te Whiti and Tohu were determined to avoid armed conflict.

The Governmental response to Parihaka, like the Waikato Kingites, was negotiation. It was not, however, a negotiation for peace at any price. At first Te Whiti was willing to accept the opening up of the land, so long as adequate reserves were defined and publicized. The Government unfortunately proceeded with the survey without detailing the reserves. In response, Te Whiti and Tohu implemented a campaign of civil disobedience. In March 1879, surveying parties were stopped, followed by the more notorious ploughing campaign in May. Throughout Taranaki, European land was ploughed up by Parihaka residents. The cabinet was forced to prepare for war. In Taranaki itself new Volunteer corps were formed with over 1,500 new recruits under training within ten days of the commencement of the ploughing campaign. This forceful demonstration, seemingly designed to

New Zealand Volunteer Officers training to defend their shore.

Fortress New Zealand: Garrison artillery training.

bolster European confidence and cower the Parihaka dissidents, was ineffectual. Ploughing continued and the settlers demanded an escalation in the government's response.

To ease tensions, the Government established a commission to investigate the Taranaki land question.Though Te Whiti refused formally to co-operate with the government's commission, his speech on 17 April 1880 to his followers was interpreted as a conciliatory one. It was less verbose than usual but its message was no less potent. It advocated living in peace and quietness in the region. In response the government recommended the development of roading on the confiscated lands using the Armed Constabulary as navvies. Nothing was taken for granted, however, and Colonel Roberts, the local commander, organised the work as a military advance. His constables moved at a cautious rate and built military encampments on the line of their advance.

When the government offered Parihaka land for sale in February 1881 and received no bids whatsoever, it became a political necessity that a solution be found to the problem. This necessity increased as 1881 progressed. Taranaki settlers, their local newspapers and politicians demanded firm action from the government, action the government would have to take if it hoped to survive in the forthcoming general election.

In response, the authorities sent a circular telegram to district commanders calling for a return of volunteers prepared to serve on the west coast. The government had finally decided to assemble an overwhelming force to march against Parihaka, a force that would intimidate any opposition. By the end of October 1881, the force converged on the plains of Rahotu only three miles from Parihaka. Consisting of nearly 1,000 volunteers and over 600 Armed Constables, this assembly was a formidable army. Thirty-three individual units from throughout the colony had by 27 October 1881 been called up for active service.

Their chance to prove themselves came on 5 November 1881. Issued with two day's rations and forty rounds of ammunition the troops formed up into a large column and marched on Parihaka. As the column closed in on Parihaka it was met not by gunfire but by singing children. Through this throng the advance party entered the centre of Parihaka seeking an assurance that its residents would desist from all further activity. When Te Whiti refused to comply, the riot act was read. At 11.30 the Armed Constabulary re-entered Parihaka and arrested Te Whiti and Tohu. They were immediately sent to New Plymouth, escorted by a squad of the Taranaki Mounted Rifles. Most perceived that Parihaka had settled the fear of a resumption of the New Zealand wars for ever. With the Maori King submitting willingly to the authority of the government and Parihaka failing to ignite the flames of War, 1881 clearly marked the demise of New Zealand's major internal security concern.

Failure of the Parihaka problem to ignite a general conflagration marked a major turning point for New Zealand defence policy. The government was able to shift its policy focus from the need to balance limited resources to protect against major threats from both within and without to concentrate more fully on the colony's external defence needs. The government, determined to carry out Scratchley's scheme, appointed a Board of officers under the chairmanship of Major-General A. G. Davidson on 1 March 1882. The board's task was to examine the rules and regulations governing the Volunteer Force and recommend any organisational restructuring required to implement Scratchley's proposals. One of the major recommendations of the Board was the appointment of a commandant, preferably of the Royal Artillery, to help overcome the unsatisfactory administration of the existing defence structure. It recommended the establishment of the existing Volunteer Force and its replacement by a totally new organisation structured along the lines advocated by Scratchley. To defend New Zealand's main harbours, the inquiry concluded that the colony required two regiments of cavalry, six regiments of Infantry and one regiment of Artillery, divided equally between the two main Islands. To be efficient administratively, the Board concluded, the twenty existing military districts should be reduced to six, three for each Island. The Board further argued for a military force divided into two divisions (lines). The 'First Line', to provide supplementation to the permanent fores stationed at the port fortifications, as well as the Field Force for mobile coast defence. The 'Second Line', to provide a reserve consisting, in the main, of country units at too great a distance from the harbours to be of immediate use. It was anticipated by the Board that the second line units would undertake a bare minimum of military training sufficient to provide a basis for further training if full scale mobilization was required. In contrast, the First line units would be expected to enrol for a minimum of three years, reside within 25 miles of their Headquarters and undertake a rigorous training regime to ensure their proficiency if called upon. In total, the Board envisaged a total force structure numbering 4,399. The First Line to consist of 2,572 while the Second Line were to number only 1,827. To train this lean force in its new role, the Board suggested that a School of Instruction and Musketry be established.

The only significant recommendation from either Scratchley or the Board's reports actioned in the short term, was the issue of a new set of general regulations. Using the draft set as a guide, the Defence Department,under the personal supervision of the Minister, arranged for the issue of a new set set of general regulations governing the Volunteer force to become effective from the 1 January 1883. Significant changes were brought about in the organisational structure, administration and training of the Volunteer force. For the first time recruits signed on for a fixed engagement, not for the three years advocated by most reforms but, for not less than one year, with three months written notice of resignation. The minimum age for general recruits was raised from 17 to 18 years old. Those who wished to join or remain in the force were expected to undergo additional training to be eligible for the capitation grant. In addition to the compulsory inspection parades, the Volunteers were required to undergo an examination in judging distances and fire two class practices on the rifle range. Officers and non-commissioned officers (NCO's) were also required to undergo additional training and testing. On top of the drill and administration examinations, officers from 1883 were required to pass examinations in minor tactics related to their particular arm. NCO's, while still appointed under 'the commanding officer's authority, were required, for the first time, to pass examinations in drill, guard duties, administration and rifle practice.

Fortress New Zealand: Preparing the gun for action.

Even the organisational structure that the Volunteers had been used to operating with changed. New divisions, foreshadowed by the persistent demands of reformers, were created. During the New Zealand War period a psychological division between the North and South Islands can be said to have existed. The 1870's had seen this division largely disappear, reflecting the slow unification of the colony's provinces into an embryonic nation. Scratchley, supported by the 1882 Board of Inquiry, recommended that a new division be instituted in the Volunteer Force; the division between coast and country. A division between those units at the main ports, who would have to face any external threat, and those in the outlying districts considered to be of no immediate utility. The 1883 regulations in essence implement this recommended division. The Volunteer Force was to be divided by two classifications, the Garrison and Country Corps. The Garrison corps were the embodiment of Scratchley's 'Fort' and 'Field Force' units and the Boards 'First Line'. They were to defend the four main ports and their immediate economic hinterlands. The Garrison Corps establishment was laid down as a minimum of 43 and a maximum of 63 volunteers. The Country corps were those recommended by Scratchley for disestablishment and by the Board for transformation into the 'Second Line.' They did not have an explicit role, though it would appear that the intent of the regulations was that they should provide a reserve if required in an emergency.

Establishment changes were not the only innovation of the 1883 regulations. The permanent staff members attached to the Volunteer Force as administrators and trainers had several alterations made to their terms of reference. For the first time it became mandatory for all correspondence to go through the Military District Office. Permanent Drill Instructors became ineligible to hold concurrent Volunteer commissions with their permanent paid employment.

An immediate result of the dramatic changes ushered in by the 1883 regulations, was the sought for reduction in the number of Volunteers. By 1884 the Volunteer Force numbered only 4,300 compared to the high of 8,000 in 1874. In the longer term, the regulations of 1883 proved to be extremely beneficial for the Volunteer Force. The provisions implemented in 1883 were not to be dramatically altered for the rest of the century. In this the regulations of 1883 provided a stability and continuity so important for any organisation. More importantly, they were judged by inspecting officers and the media to have instigated a new age of disciplined training that would lead to a marked improvement in the efficiency and usefulness of New Zealand's Volunteer Force.

The foundations laid by the 1883 regulations and Scratchley's report were to be built upon over the next six years by governments influenced by Sir William Francis Drummond Jervois. Jervois, the military mentor of Scratchley, was appointed as Governor of New Zealand in December 1882 and arrived in the colony in

January 1883 to take up his new office. While an experienced Governor, having served in the Straits settlement and South Australia, Jervois was primarily a defence consultant for colonial governments who saw it as his duty to advise his ministers on defence. For the six years preceding his arrival in New Zealand he had been engaged with Scratchley on devising schemes for the defence of Australia.

As soon as he arrived in the country, Jervois expressed his determination to take up the defence question and offered his military expertise to the government who were more than willing to have his advice. Within three months of becoming Governor, he had visited and examined the ports of Wellington, Auckland, Lyttelton, Port Chalmers and the Bluff. Realising that Scratchley's initial work had been conceptual Jervois noted that it was essential that a more detailed plan be devised. Unfortunately Scratchley was over-committed and could not personally do the task, so Jervois suggested that the government apply for the services of another experienced engineering officer. Again the government was happy to accept Jervois' advice and went so far as to allow him to arrange the application for a suitable officer. Having already decided what type of defence works New Zealand required, Jervois sought, with Scratchley's assistance, a competent officer to supervise the detailed execution of his plan. Major Cautley, another of Jervois' understudies, was sent by the Imperial authorities and after consulting with Scratchley en route, arrived in New Zealand, briefed to recommend works devised by the Governor.

Though able to obtain the services of a well qualified engineering officer, neither the governor nor the government was able to secure the services of a currently serving Imperial officer to take up the appointment of commandant. As a result the government offered the post to Colonel George Stoddart Whitmore. Whitmore had proved himself, not only on the battlefield, but also on the Treasury benches. Before he was able to take up his new appointment, a unique piece of legislation had to be drafted and passed through Parliament. As a member of the Legislative Council, Whitmore would normally have vacated his seat on taking up the post of commandant. However, Whit–

more insisted that he be able to return to politics and a compromise was found with the 'Whitmore Enabling Act of 1885'. Under its provisions, Whitmore was permitted to retain his Legislative Council seat as well as hold the office of commander of New Zealand's defence forces so long as he did not sit in the chamber or vote in any of its divisions.

Once the Enabling Act had become law Whitmore, promoted to Major-General, took up his post and began work on improving the efficiency of New Zealand's defence forces. It would be easy to make exaggerated claims with regard to the importance of the new commandant. On the surface at least, his reforms appear both substantial and all embracing. Whitmore was after all the commandant who was to establish a School of Military Instruction; it was he who insisted on elected officers passing commission examinations three months after their appointment, and it was he who arranged for the establishment of Honorary Reserve Corps as a method of disbanding corps stationed too distant from ports to be of immediate use. Yet none of what Whitmore implemented was novel or innovative. The 1882 Board of Inquiry had identified the need for a Military School, while the 1883 Regulations required officers within six months of their appointment to pass prescribed commissioning examinations. Scratchley in his 1880 report and the 1882 Boards report had both recommended the disbanding of country units, with the 1882 Board of Inquiry recommending that they be incorporated into the reservist second line. While Whitmore was not important for originality, he was still an important appointee; his importance lay in his ability to refine, consolidate and, most importantly, implement existing policy proposals.

Capitalising on the renewal of interest in defence, Whitmore hastened construction of the fortifications already commenced by Cautley for the four main ports, organised administrative battalions for volunteer corps and arranged for the passage of a new Defence Act through parliament in 1886. The new Act, for the first time, regulated all the branches of New Zealand's Defence Forces under one law and transformed the Armed Constabulary into the Police Force and Permanent Militia. In the same year that the Defence Act was passed, Whitmore issued yet

Major General Whitmore: New Zealand's first Commandant.

another new set of regulations for the control of the Volunteer Force.

1887 should have been the year of fruition for Whitmore's reforms. The administrative battalions and brigades had been in place for two years, the Defence Act of 1886 had been law for one and his revision of the regulations became effective on 1 January. Yet this year was to mark the beginning of the end. The economy went into a major recession and demands for retrenchment in government spending were heard throughout the colony.

Following the lead of both the New South Wales and Victorian governments, the New Zealand Minister of Defence invited Major-General H. Schaw to review and report on the colony's defence. Having been briefed to reduce expenditure to its lowest, Schaw reconsidered the question of New Zealand's defence needs within limited means. Consulting Whitmore and his staff, Schaw was able to ascertain the existing forces available for defence and form an opinion as to the absolute minimum required to protect the colony, and to argue that, since the struggles with the interior Maori tribes had ceased it was a waste of money to maintain any force for internal defence. New Zealand was still, however, liable to attack from external foes determined to obtain money, coals and stores as well as inflict injury and humiliation on a portion of the British Empire. Having accepted Scratchley's basic premises, Schaw went on to accept that New Zealand, like any nation with an extended seaboard, was unable to provide defence for the whole coast-line. To be both efficient and effective, defence resources had to be concentrated on the vital points, the main harbours. For minor seaport towns such as Nelson, New Plymouth and the like Schaw suggested that rifle clubs, which encouraged the art of shooting, and honorary Volunteer Corps could provide the semblance of a military presence. For Auckland, Wellington, Lyttelton and Dunedin a minimum force of 4,314 was required consisting of 343 Permanent Militia and 3,982 Volunteers. As the Volunteers numbered 8,403 at the time of Schaw's review, he was advocating a reduction of 4,421. More important for the government than the reduction in numbers was the savings in expenditure. Schaw's scheme would save approximately £27,500. While Schaw advocated a reduction in quantity, he bal–

anced this by stressing the need for quality. The Garrison Coast Brigade Volunteers, for example, would, under Schaw's re-organisation, be required to undergo more advance training in the special duties of serving heavy guns, laying submarine mines and long torpedoes. When reviewed by the Imperial 'Colonial Defence Committee' in April 1888 Schaw's plan was complimented and his proposed reductions and alterations considered justified.

In the grips of a major economic depression and needing to curtail costs, the government happily accepted Schaw's recommendations. It also accepted the resignation of Major-General Whitmore as commandant. For the government, Whitmore's resignation was a golden opportunity to save more money and his position was allowed to remain vacant, with the under-secretary of defence acting as a defacto commandant. Non-replacement of Whitmore was not the only cost saving measure pursued by the government in the field of defence. The central School of Instruction and the administrative battalion structure were abolished, while the practice of issuing free railway passes to volunteers on duty was discontinued.

Over the next three years defence suffered as a consequence of the economic downturn. This was to be reversed in 1891 when the liberals took the Treasury benches and Richard John Seddon the defence portfolio. Surprisingly, one of Seddon's first acts was further retrenchment. After a hurried tour of inspection of the colony's defence establishments, Seddon dismissed an under secretary, three Lieutenant-Colonels and several junior officers, making a further saving of £4,800 per annum in salaries. Seddon was not, however, simply trying to save money. His obvious intent was to have his department run as efficiently and economically as possibly. As soon as he had completed his disestablishment of positions, he regarded as surplus Seddon devolved decision making to the lowest possible level and emphasised to the remaining employees that they were regarded as efficient and faithful servants. In response, those still on the defence pay roll were credited with working with more will, confidence and vigour.

With his ministry refashioned to meet his needs, Seddon set about revitalising the Volunteer Force. To make the force more professional, Seddon wished to see an Imperial officer, conversant with modern military ideas, appointed for a five year term as commandant. Such an appointee, Seddon believed, would bring the requisite expertise to help upgrade and reinvigorate the Volunteer Force. Secondly, to ensure that the best candidates available rose to lead the country's volunteer units, Seddon proposed to replace the 'bottom-up' elective system of officer selection with a 'top-down' nomination system. The new system was to be controlled by the new commandant using the services of the officers commanding the military districts. Seddon also proposed changes to the funding formula for governmental capitation. Instead of a yearly grant apportioned by Parliament, Seddon argued for a three year guaranteed minimum capitation to enable units to make long term financial committments without fear of overtaxing their resources.

Success in his endeavours seemed to come in 1892, when approval was given for the appointment of Lieutenant Colonel F. J. Fox to the post of commandant of the New Zealand Defence Forces. On his arrival Fox appeared to be the saviour the Defence Force was looking for. Instead of formally taking up his appointment Fox obtained the Premier's permission to travel the length and breadth of the country on a tour of inspection. Over a nine month period Fox examined all of New Zealand's installations, units and their officers, seeking out their strengths and exposing their weaknesses for scrutiny. This immediate show of dynamism on the new commandant's part, while ultimately resulting in significant improvements to New Zealand Defence forces initially unleashed a major political controversy.

The controversy was prompted by the publication in June 1893 of Fox's inspection report on the state of the colony's defences. Submitted in three parts between February and June 1893 the report was one of most thorough inspections ever undertaken of New Zealand's defences. Best described as a condemnation of the existing system, Fox's report was to result in a polarisation of both debate and public opinion on defence issues for the next three years. This result was exactly what Fox seemed determined

Mobile Field Force under training.

to achieve, as he believed the previous system of reporting was inaccurate, indeed incompetent. Such reporting, he believed, had lulled the colony into believing its defence forces were more efficient than they in fact were. He saw it as his "...imperative duty to dispel that belief..." In carrying out this self appointed task Fox, in clear and uncompromising language, highlighted the deficiencies of New Zealand's whole defence establishment. Only one unit, the Otago Hussars was in Fox's estimation efficient. Fox went on to rub salt into the wound he had opened by commenting on all Volunteer Officers individually. Of the two hundred and sixty-four commissioned officers serving at the time of his inspection Fox was able to classify one hundred and ninety-six (seventy-five percent) as fair to very good. The remaining sixty-eight officers he damned as indifferent or bad.

In an endeavour to overcome the shortcomings of the Volunteer force, Fox argued that the existing regulations governing the force should be revised. For the defence of the colony, Fox believed a totally new defence scheme had to be evolved to meet the current need. Fox's planned defence scheme, as with previous proposals, was designed to provide the colony with adequare defence at minimum cost. Fox noted that for defence planning two conditions existed, either Britain retained supremacy of the seas and New Zealand, along with the rest of the Empire, remained fundamentally secure, or alternatively the British navy could not command the sea lanes and the Empire was lost, vulnerable to unannounced attack by any maritime aggressor. To counter effectively the likely low level threats to the colony's security, Fox proposed a major restructuring of defence organisation and administration. After carefully examining the colony's fourteen Military districts in both Islands, Fox recommended that they be reduced by amalgamation to four major districts centred on Auckland, Wellington, Christchurch and Dunedin, together with one minor district based on Nelson-Westland. (It was not until February 1895 that this reduction in the aministrative districts actually occurred). Fox argued that such radical restructuring would help concentrate defence efforts on the most likely targets of any attack, the four main centres and the strategic coal reserves of West Port. To defend each of these new districts

New Zealand Volunteers parading in full dress.

Fox advocated major changes to both the Garrison and Field force units. Fox, on completion of his tour of inspection, carefully assessed the minimum manpower and equipment requirements to defend each district he had proposed. For Wellington he believed a 1228 man force, 1111 (ninety percent) of whom were to be Volunteers was needed. In Auckland he proposed a 1075 man force of whom 990 were to be Volunteers. Further south in Dunedin Fox argued that the district required a 1127 man force comprised of sixty-four permanent militia and 1063 Volunteers, while in Christchurch fifty-six permanent militia and 987 Volunteers were needed for its defence. Across the Ranges in the smaller district of Nelson and Westland he believed one hundred and ninety-one men, of whom only two were to be permanent staff, should be able to protect the important coal reserves. The colony's volunteers, under the scheme proposed by Fox, would number only 4,340 approximately two thousand less than were at that time enrolled. To make the necessary manpower savings Fox recommended the disbandment of forty-one (40 percent) of the existing one hundred and two units. In the main, these units were country corps which Fox believed were of little immediate use and were thus a drain on the limited financial and material resources available for defence in New Zealand.

To make the most efficient use of resources available Fox argued in favour of an armament replacement programme, changes to training programmes as well as organisational re-structuring. The worn out, unserviceable and often dangerous Snider rifles, Fox argued, must be replaced immediately. Fox noted that New Zealand appeared incapable of training its troops effectively. The officers were unskilled commanders, in-capable of acting as instructors and the permanent force instructors were out of date, over worked and as a consequence, generally inefficient. Fox argued that for training to improve, the government would have to appoint at least six additional Imperial Staff officers and instructors. To give encouragement to individual volunteers Fox urged the government to increase capitation as well as provide personal bonuses for Volunteers attending encampments of three or more days. Individual training by itself was not, however, sufficient. Individual efficiency had to be harnessed and to do this Fox recommended that units be organised into higher formations. Noting that the Artillery corps had already been organised into a single regiment Fox proposed to join together the independent Infantry and Mounted Units into battalions. With such a structure manned by well equipped and trained troops, Fox was confident the nation could defend itself against low level threats. However, he was adamant that his proposals be seen as an integrated scheme that could not have its individual components tampered with. As he himself said:

> "...all the recommendations are intimately connected, and the cutting out of one or the reducing of any of the expenditure proposed will at once alter the whole scheme..."

Purely as a scheme of defence for the colony, the proposals put forward by Fox were well conceived. When they were critically examined by two other military experts with experience in New Zealand, Jervois and Schaw, they along with the author were praised. Fox's scheme was also economic; if carried out it would have resulted not only in immediate improvements in defence preparedness, it would also have saved money. Though the proposed scheme was cost effective, it did not receive unanimous support in the legislature or the colony. Fox, though an able military officer, was an inept politician. His attacks on individual officers and units when made public unleashed an unparalleled controversy in the history of the defence debate in New Zealand.

The two opposing views on Fox and his report were expressed vehemently in Parliament and press. Taking sides the media took the controversy to the people. Those newspapers which opposed the report and especially the adverse reporting of the 68 officers, titled them "Fox's Martyrs". Unfortunately the media supporters of Fox were unable to come up with such an emotive catch phrase. Attacked both in the press and in Parliament, Fox decided to resign. His resignation, in fact, came before he had officially taken up his appointment as commandant. Though he resigned as commandant, Fox remained as the Government's military advisor. His report had highlighted defence weaknesses that all recognised needed to be addressed.To address these weaknesses, Seddon called together a conference of 22 selected officers, including Fox, to discuss defence. This conference, under the chairmanship of Whitmore, met in Wellington for eleven days during late September and early October 1894. The recommendations of the conference,numbering only twenty-six in total, were a summary of those made by almost every inspector of New Zealand defences.

As soon as the conference submitted its findings, Seddon commenced an intimate study of their recommendations on regulations, with a view to incorporating them into the set he was working on, as well as making any amendments to legislation that were necessary.Within five months Seddon, with Fox's assistance, was able to promulgate a revised set of defence regulations and have amending legislation ready for submission to Parliament for approval. The regulations themselves were gazetted on 28 February 1895 to come into force on 1 March of that year. In form, they were almost identical to the preceding sets of well over a decade. The only discernible change, in line with the recommendations of both Fox and the Volunteer officers conference, was made to establishments. All units, except Naval or Garrison Artillery, were to be allowed a maximum of sixty and a minimum of forty personnel. For Naval and Garrison Artillery Units the maximum was to be 100 with the minimum being sixty. For each of the four districts, Auckland, Wellington, Christchurch and Dunedin, an establishment of 790 men was laid down. These establishments were to consist of 1 Mounted Corps, 3 Naval or Garrison Artillery Corps, 1 Field Artillery Corps, 1 Engineer Corps, a Rifle Corps and a Garrison Band.

The immediate result of the restructuring and implementation of changes recommended by Fox and the Volunteer officer conference, was a marked improvement in New Zealand's defence capability. Taking the opportunity of the discernible improvement in the state of New Zealand's military forces and the return of Lieutenant-Colonel Fox to the United Kingdom Seddon, on 22 June 1896, handed over the defence portfolio to Thomas Thompson. To replace Fox the Liberal ministry once again asked the War Office, through the Governor, to provide a suitable officer to command the colony's forces. In response to this request the War Office recommended Major Arthur Pole Penton, like Fox, a highly regarded artillery officer. The War Office's nominee was accepted and Penton was offered, and accepted, the appointment of commandant for five years. Arriving in late 1896, Penton was gazetted in his new appointment and quietly began to assess the colony's defence requirements and how they were being met.

Like all his predecessors, Penton had some major concerns after reviewing the colony's defences. He argued that defence preparations consisted of much more than purchasing guns, torpedoes, associated equipment and constructing strong em-placements and fortifications. From his own inspection of the forces in early 1897 he perceived several deficiencies that required to be remedied immediately. If action was not taken, the colony

Fortress New Zealand: Artillery training.

Fortress New Zealand: Observing the fall of shot.

would be forced to rely for its security on a Volunteer Force that was not only inefficient, but also inappropriate for its role. According to Penton, the force undertook insufficient and inadequate training for its officers and men. It lacked an essential feature of all defence forces, a practised and experienced higher command; worst of all it, could not function for any prolonged period in the field as it had no logistics tail or medical support services

While Penton had a clearly defined policy plan to instill military professionalism into, what he considered, the colony's inadequate defence forces, by itself this would not have achieved anything. His itemisation of the defences of the forces was not novel nor were his solutions. Penton, however, like Major-General Whitmore, was to be extremely fortunate in the timing of his appointment. 1897 was to see the commencement of a major revival of interest in New Zealand's Defence Forces. For New Zealand, and indeed the whole of the British Empire, 1897 was to be the year of the 'Diamond Jubilee'. A year marked by celebrations and monuments to Victoria, who at seventy-eight had been Queen of England, Defender of the Faith, Empress of India and ruler of the British Dominions beyond the seas for a record sixty years. To ensure that the record reign would not be forgotten, the Imperial authorities invited the colonies to send military contingents to the planned public commemorations ceremonies in London in mid-June. In response to this invitation, New Zealand sent a fifty-four strong contingent, the first colonially raised military contingent to leave its shores. The importance of the contingent to the development of New Zealand's Defence Forces was out of all proportion to its size. Not only did it assist in raising public awareness of New Zealand's Volunteer Force, it also provided a model for mobilization, training, selection and despatch of military contingents. A model that was to be well used over the succeeding five years.

The involvement of the Volunteer Force in supplying men for the 'Jubilee Contingent', was to have a profound effect. General interest in defence and the Volunteer force was revived after years of public indifference. The Defence Department was in–

undated with offers of service of new corps from throughout the colony.

The year 1898 was a further year of promise and progress for defence. New Zealand's citizens, Penton was glad to observe, had finally begun to take a genuine interest in the military position of the colony. They desired to see their politicians and military advisors put ' the defences and the forces of the colony into a trustworthy and efficient state'. The newspapers, aware of the renewed interest, pioneered the concept of defence being a national non-party issue. All peoples and politicians should strive to ensure a proper scheme for the defence of the state, a call that politicians heard and quickly acted on. Impetus for the growing interest in the colony's defences was not simply a flow-on from that generated by Jubilee fever. It was the result of internal as well as international conflicts and conquests. The first, and probably least significant, was the so called 'Dog Tax War' in Northland. Hone Toia of the Mahurehure hapu of the Ngapuhi lead a disgruntled group of Maori determined to oppose the dog tax levied by the Hokianga county. In response, the central gov–

New Zealand Volunteers at rest — Easter camp.

ernment sent a detachment of one hundred and twenty men of the Permanent Militia under the command of Lieutenant Newall to maintain the peace. At the same time arrangements were made to raise an expeditionary force of one hundred picked men from the Volunteer units of Auckland.

Of greater importance for the growth in interest in the colony's defences was the marked growth in international tension. The need for Britain to join with other powers in defensive alliances was highlighted for New Zealanders at least, by the success of the United States in its war against Spain in 1898. It was not that the United States directly threatened the nation's security, more it was the lesson it hammered home. Spain had been defeated relatively quickly without once being attacked in its European homeland. All attacks had been directed at her most vulnerable points, her colonies and dependencies. For the few in New Zealand who viewed the colony's isolation as adequate protection, the American success was a shattering experience. For the majority who had always seen New Zealand as vulnerable by its distance from Britain and its dependence on the sea lanes, America's success was yet another timely reminder. If Great Britain were to go to war with a European adversary she, like Spain, would be attacked at its most vulnerable points, her far flung colonies, like New Zealand. Realising this, civic leaders were quick to demand that the central government upgrade the colony's coastal defences.

In response to the growing awareness of New Zealand's vulnerability, its colonists once again took the trouble to organise themselves into Volunteer units. In 1898 no fewer than seventy-one proposed Volunteer Corps sought permission from the Defence Department for formation. The government, in an apparent attempt to foster the revival of interest in defence, approved a new establishment for the Volunteer force which allowed capitation to be paid to a total of 7,000 men, which, according to Penton, effectively meant the force could expand up to 8,000 men when non-efficients were taken into account. Attempting to maximize the potential benefits from the revival, the government, through a defence committee in conjunction with senior military officers, re-examined and inspected the country's defences and completed the drawing up of a defence scheme. Penton had commenced preparation for the defence scheme in 1897 on his arrival in the colony. In it, all key installations and how they were to be defended were identified. Units were given responsibility for specific tasks and were also informed on how they were to mobilize in case of emergency.

This revised scheme, however, was quickly outdated. Events in South Africa were to overshadow New Zealand's local defence preparations. The mentality of 'Fortress New Zealand' was to be replaced by forward defence. New Zealand was to become a full participant in the British defence alliance with its provision of contingents for service on the veldt.

Chapter Four:

THE SOUTH AFRICAN WAR

The Boer or Afrikaaner inhabitants of Southern Africa, trace their origins back to Dutch, French and German Huguenot settlers of the mid 17th century. By the mid 19th century they had become a rugged, self-sufficient and independent people at odds with the British settlers and in conflict with African tribes. When the British government assumed the administration of the Cape Colony following the Napoleonic Wars, a large number of Boers set out on their Great Trek to the north. There they founded two Boer republics, the Orange Free State and the Transvaal, but there was to be no escape from further clashes of interest and problems of sovereignty with Britain, clashes that would event–ually lead to war.

The first clash of arms went well for the Boers. Under the com–mand of Major General Sir George Colley, Britain sent, in 1880-1881, an expeditionary force tasked with annexing the Transvaal. The campaign was badly managed and the British were soundly defeated at Majuba Hill and forced to withdraw, leaving the Boer government intact and the British inhabitants of South Africa dismayed.

When gold was discovered in the Transvaal, its problems multiplied as foreigners (Uitlanders), mostly British, poured in. Soon outnumbering the original Boer inhabitants, the Uitlanders demanded the right to vote and changes in the laws and taxation. A misguided attempt to assert Uitlander claims by force - the ill-fated Jameson raid of 1895 - was easily crushed. Tension rose as the threatened Boers, with the encouragement of European powers, resisted British demands and strengthened their armouries. In September 1899, the Transvaal Boers began mobilising and most Uitlanders fled the country. War seemed inevitable. The British Government was as resolved upon confrontation as their Boer counterparts. British subjects everywhere, they asserted, had a right to protection. The severity of Boer rule, including their attitude towards the blacks, was condemned. Boer intransigence and arrogance hardened British attitudes, and support for settlement of the dispute by resort to arms if necessary was overwhelming in Britain and its self-governing colonies. The Boers were no less willing to take up arms. They anticipated foreign intervention on their behalf, overlooking in this respect the importance of British sea power, and believed that Britain would shrink back from the effort in lives, time and money that would be required to defeat them.

War began on 11 October 1899, between Transvaal and Britain with the Orange Free State immediately joining their Boer kith and kin. At first the Boers held the initiative. Although liked by his men, General Sir Redvers Buller, the first British commander, was hesitant and irresolute, in the habit of changing his mind at the height of battle and blaming others for defeats. British tactics were rigid and unimaginative, seeking formal, almost set piece, battles. Their enemy was more flexible. Magnificent horsemen and familiar with the country, they became adept at harassment and irregular warfare. Within months the British were besieged at Ladysmith, Mafeking and Kimberley, and had suffered defeats at Magersfontein, Stormberg and Colenso.

On the British side, firmer direction was obviously needed. In January 1900 Field Marshal Lord Roberts took over the command of British forces, with General (later Lord) Kitchener as his chief of staff. As British troops and supplies built up, and the Boers remained fundamentally defensive in their strategy, the British position steadily improved. Roberts was soon in a position to take the offensive. While Boer forces in east and west were held, strong British columns advanced on a broad front northwards from Cape Colony, rolling up the Boer centre. The plan worked

Raising the funds and troops to fight.

admirably and the Boer capitals were both soon in British hands. The besieged towns were relieved and the Boer leader, Cronjé, captured with 5000 of his troops. Within a year of the beginning of hostilities, the end seemed in sight and the British confidently expected an early peace. Roberts returned to England, leaving Kitchener to wind up the operations.

But the Boers refused to give up, and the war took on a more bitter aspect as they turned to guerilla tactics, attacking British rail supplies, blockhouses and isolated columns. A series of brilliant raids inspired Boer resistance. Kitchener's response was two-fold: he sought first, to reduce the scope of guerilla operations by establishing lines of blockhouses and, second, to remove the sources of food and shelter available to the Boer commandos.

The country was gradually cleared of people and stock. Farms were destroyed and the Boer population moved into concentration camps, where atrocious conditions caused many deaths, especially among children. This policy was not initially successful, for the Boers under arms, thus relieved of the need to provide for their dependents, had their hands freed, but the removal of their means of sustenance and the continuing British military operations finally began to have effect. On 31 May 1902 the hungry, ragged and ill-armed Boer remnants accepted the inevitable and surrendered at Vereeniging. Throughout the whole of the South African conflict New Zealand was to be an active participant on the side of Britain.

On 28 September 1899, two weeks before war was declared, Seddon sought approval from Parliament to offer a New Zealand contingent for service with the British Army in the Transvaal. Seconded by the leader of the parliamentary opposition, Russell (who was actually sympathetic to the Boer position), the proposal gained overwhelming support. In the House, the vote was fifty-four to five in favour, while in the council it was thirty-six to one. In less than a month, the Imperial authorities had accepted New Zealand's offer and the first contingent of 214 men was despatched to establish a worthy fighting tradition. When the contingent left Wellington on 21 October 1899, it was farewelled by an enthusiastic crowd of between forty and sixty thousand well wishers. To the immense delight of all New Zealand, this force was the first colonial contingent to arrive at Captetown in late November. The enthusiasm shown for the departing contingent was in the space of two months transferred to the ballot box. In 1899, Seddon once again had to face the electorate and to his, and the opposition's, astonishment he was swept back to power with a majority of 30 when it was previously predicted he would lose. The results of the December poll were chiefly attributed to the decision to despatch a New Zealand contingent for service in Transvaal. New Zealanders, it seemed, were more than happy with the governments endeavours to strengthen Imperial bonds by way of an active military alliance.

Given a clear mandate from the public, Seddon was more than willing to give further assistance to Britain after the gloomy news

South Africa: Artillery preparing for war.

South Africa: Officers prepare.

of 'Black Week' reached the colony. This week of military disasters that befell the Imperial Forces in Southern Africa between 9 and 15 December 1899 strengthened Imperial resolve to defeat the Boer commandos. Immediately following 'Black Week' New Zealand's first contingent, with only rudimentary training, was thrown into action firing its first shots in anger on 18 December. At the same time in New Zealand, preparations were commenced to send a second contingent. Sailing on 20 January 1900 the second contingent reached South Africa late in the following month. This was followed over the next two years by a further eight contingents. In total 6,495 men, together with 8,000 horses, were to serve in the war. As New Zealand's commitment to the war increased, its ability to provide trained men decreased. These first two contingents consisted almost entirely of men from New Zealand's existing Volunteer Force. As further contingents were required, more and more men had to be recruited from those without any previous military training. Increasingly the only criteria used for selection were the ability to ride and shoot straight.

While the war was being conducted on the veldt, New Zealand's Volunteer Force was suffering at home due to the large scale commitment of men, material and time to the departing contingents. The commitment to the war effort meant that much needed administrative support and instructional staff were unavailable to meet the ongoing demands of the Volunteer Force. All readily acknowledging the short term disadvantages to the Volunteers, and noting they would continue for as long as New Zealand had its commitment to South Africa, it was however argued by politicians and senior members of the Defence Department that the predicted long term benefits would make it all worthwhile.

Exacerbating the problems of a Volunteer Force bereft of permanent staff support, was the massive expansion it experienced. In one year alone, 1899 to 1900, the Force swelled by sixty-three percent (7,000 to 11,444 enrolled members). This explosive expansion threatened to snap the already overly stretched defence infrastructure. Lack of staff meant that some newly raised country units had no provision for training. The same lack meant that no worthwhile training could be undertaken at encampments notable only for their record attendances. For Colonel Penton, the commandant, this situation, while posing a major problem, also provided more useful ammunition for his campaign to have the School of Instruction re-established. Determined that the Force continue to increase its field training, Penton argued that the best way of overcoming staff shortages was to train the Volunteer Force command element at a central School of Instruction. With defence issues being politically popular it is not surprising that Penton's desire for the re-establishment of the central school was finally taken up in Parliament. Considered a popular as well as beneficial measure, agreement was reached to have the School re-established.

Acceptance, albeit belatedly, for the need of a School of Instruction by New Zealand's politicians was another manifestation of the general growth of interest and awareness of defence by Parliament. Another indication of this growing interest was the decision by the Premier, Seddon, to renew his personal association with the Defence Department. On 23 January 1900 he once again took responsibility for the defence portfolio. A third indication that defence was an issue worthy of attention was the instigation of yet another review of the colony's security precautions and preparations. This review was initiated by a defence statement tabled by Seddon in July. It was undertaken by a Joint Defence Committee formed from both Houses given the task of investigating all matters affecting the defence of the colony. Prompting this activity by the legislative were two basic factors. The first, obviously, was the war being waged on the veldt. The second was the resurgence in Britain, with a consequential spill-over to New Zealand, of invasion paranoia. A paranoia fuelled by British regular troops being withdrawn from the homeland for service in Southern Africa. In his July defence statement, Seddon intimated that he believed the defence forces of the colony should be expanded in both size and scope. He believed that they should also be divided into five categories; the Permanent Artillery, the ordinary Volunteers, an Imperial Reserve Force for service with British Regulars, Rifle Clubs and the Cadet Corps. Using Seddon's vision as a guide, the Joint Defence Committee reviewed current policy and had its report ready by August. In it, the committee recommended that all offers of service by prospective Volunteer corps be accepted. For New Zealand's volunteers this meant further expansion. The overtaxed Defence Department had to organise the growth of the Volunteer Force from an already swelled establishment of 11,444 in one hundred and fifty units to 17,000 in two hundred and thirty.

Support for the continued expansion of New Zealand's Volunteer Force was not universal. Some members of the parliamentary opposition, for example, were quick to point out that defence was not improved by putting numbers on rolls. The increase in numbers they noted was not paralleled by an increase in the number of competent officers or non-commissioned officers. Rather than simply increasing the number of corps in the establishment, it would be better, they argued, to increase the maximum number allowed for existing corps. This, it was hoped, would mean that key personnel would at least know the rudiments of their Military work. It was also questioned whether an increase in the size of the Volunteer Force should occur. Many, including Russell and Penton, believed that New Zealand's strategic situation had not changed from those outlined by Scratchley in 1881. It would be, therefore, cheaper and more effective if a large contribution was made to the Royal Navy rather than financing an expansion of the local Volunteer Force, a force which they believed would have little utility if New Zealand found itself at war. Opposition to the planned expansion of the Volunteer Force was however unsuccessful. Seddon, the main architect of expansion, had perceived that the enthusiasm shown by the public for volunteering was an outward or physical manifestation of patriotism, a patriotism that was sweeping the country as a result of interest and support for the South African War. It was also a spirit that had secured the treasury benches for his ministry in 1899 and he was determined to foster it for political reasons.

In addition to sending contingents to South Africa to fight, New Zealand sent two contingents to Australia. One of seventy-three mounted rifles, to take part in the Federation celebrations. The other, consisting of two hundred and fourteen representatives from all arms, to take part in the celebrations marking the open–

South Africa: Resting after the long trek.

South Africa: A Sergeant of the 5th Contingency.

ing of the first Federal Parliament in Melbourne. In Australia a combined Imperial and Indian Army contingent had also taken part in the Federation celebrations. On the invitation of the New Zealand government this combined contingent took the opportunity to visit the colony. While here, they put on splendid military demonstrations from one end of the country to the other. Penton hoped that for the total cost of £4,000 required to transport, accommodate and feed them, their presence would raise the spirit of rivalry within New Zealand's Defence Forces as well as provide a standard to emulate.

The standard set by the Imperial and Indian forces was soon matched. During the visit of the Duke and Duchess of Cornwall and York a spectacular review was held in Christchurch on 24 June 1901. Four hundred and thirty officers, seven thousand three hundred and thirty five men and two thousand nine hundred cadets came together from throughout both Islands in the largest muster of men under arms ever held in the colony. Then, on a small scale, the scene was repeated at each district headquarters the royal couple visited.

While the Duke and Duchess of Cornwall and York's visit was a joyous occasion that practised New Zealand's Volunteers in massed mobilisation, the other royal happening of 1901 was mournful. On 22 January 1901 Queen Victoria had finally succumbed to death. Queen Victoria's demise was almost symbolic, a symbolism matched by the transitional nature of 1901 for the Volunteers of New Zealand. At the end of the year they were to see not only a new monarch, but also a new commandant. Penton was to to be replaced by a South African war veteran, Major-General James Melville Babington. Babington was highly regarded, not only as a thinker, but also as a tactician; the colony looked forward to his arrival.

Babington officially took command of the forces on 23 January 1902. Though a new commandant, in a new year, with a new monarch on the throne, Babington faced the same problems as his predecessor. Babington, as Penton and so many before him, noted that the greatest weakness of New Zealand's Defence Forces was their training. Like Penton, Babington wished to see more outdoor training, with musketry practised at unknown

Royal visitors witnessed a spectacular review.

ranges. He also wished to see progressive formation training, starting with the smallest unit and working up, to ensure that all levels of command were capable of fulfilling their roles in the field. To maximise the use of training resources, Babington scrapped, what he considered, the wasteful Easter Encampments. In their place, he wished to see unit training corps, conducted by officers and non-commissioned officers who had undertaken courses at the Central School of Instruction. Though in 1902 Babington faced the same basic problems as his predecessors, it was also definitely the end of an era. Not only was a new king crowned but the South African War was concluded.

Casualties:

During the war, 288 New Zealanders died. 59 of whom were killed in active service, the remainder dying as a result of accident and disease. In addition 166 New Zealanders were wounded.

New Zealand Mounted Riflemen on the way to Bulawayo.

Chapter Five:

AN IMPERIAL ARMY

At the end of the South African War much debate was generated on what defence preparations New Zealand actually needed for its security. Babington believed that the only way to have an effective defence was to concentrate forces at vulnerable points. In contrast, some politicians argued that the only effective defence was the creation of a nation of marksmen able to defend the country in the same manner as the Boers had done in South Africa. To mediate between the opposing views it was decided to establish a Council of Defence based on the British model. The New Zealand Council consisted of the Defence Minister, the Chief of General Staff, a Finance Minister and a Secretary. New Zealand's Council, working in combination with the Council of Defence of Great Britain, was tasked not only with organising forces for home defence and for any overseas commitment that might arise. Other tasks devolved to the Council were, firstly, the formulation of regulations that would make the forces more popular as well as encourage enlistment and efficiency. Secondly, the decentralisation of command and control of the forces.

The council immediately proceeded to fulfill its duties as best it could. Between 1907 and 1909 it revoked 71 regulations, made an additional 81 and amended a further 238 in its endeavours to encourage New Zealand's Volunteer system. To implement the government's wish of decentralized control of the forces, the Council gave District Commanders more authority and respon–

sibility over their districts. The Council also prepared regulations and instructions for mobilization, designed to assemble and equip, at short notice, Military Units and mould them into an effective force capable of resisting low level attacks. The Council's mobilization plans were greatly assisted by technological developments and hindered by organisational deficiencies. Concentration of mobilized forces by horse and harness was vastly improved by the completion in the North Island of the main trunk line. It was hindered, however, by the continued absence of an 'Army Service Corps' able to provide logistical back-up to the forces and essential if an army wished to survive on the battlefield.

Following the path pioneered by Imperial commandants, the Council aligned the training of New Zealand defence forces more closely with the British Regular Army. Imperial training manuals and instructional pamphlets were purchased and used for training New Zealand's forces. To assist with the implementation of the more Imperially aligned training, instruction staff visited each district. The training organised by the council was obviously designed to reinforce Imperial links and ensure that any contingent sent from New Zealand would be able to take its place in an envisaged 'Homogeneous Imperial Army'. It also provided for expansion of the force due to either increased popular support or governmental direction.

The Council was also instrumental in moving the nation toward accepting compulsory military service for its citizens. On 7 August 1907, the Council submitted a damning report on New Zealand's Defence Forces. On the first page of this report a warning was given to the nation that: "...should the Volunteer Force not be maintained or brought up to an efficient state, volunteering has had its last chance. If the general public are in earnest as to defence, they must themselves assist and ensure that under the Volunteer system sufficient enlistment is made, and that once men are enlisted they attend regularly. The alternative is a system of universal or compulsory training, whereby the burden of service in the Defence Forces will be more evenly distributed..."

Eventually New Zealand accepted compulsory military service because of the Council's warning and the activities of the well organised pressure group the 'National Defence League'. The League seized opportunities to play on the fears of the people. Established on 25 August 1906 the Defence League wished to:

> "...create a sentiment which would induce the patriots of the land to bind themselves together for the creation of an efficient force to look after the interests of the country in case of conflict..."

Specifically, it wished to see the introduction of compulsory military training based on the Swiss concept of every citizen a soldier. By 1907 the campaign organised by the Defence League was gathering momentum, enlisting the support of men from all

An Imperial Army: Kitchener visits New Zealand.

ranks and professions, including the Prime Minister, and had launched a journal entitled "Defence" to spread its views. The members of the National Defence League of New Zealand were also conscious of Imperial needs. 1907 had seen the establishment of the Imperial General Staff. Born out of the 1907 Colonial Conference, the Imperial General Staff was tasked with the responsibility of combining the autonomous forces of the Empire into a homogeneous Imperial Army in an emergency.

After the Imperial General Staff was established the National Defence League of New Zealand stepped up its campaign. In addition to publishing its views through "Defence", the League took an active part in politics. During the 1908 general election campaign, League members questioned all candidates on their views on military training and those views were then made public. In addition, public meetings with well informed speakers were organised throughout the country to heighten public awareness. Two important speakers for the campaign were Colonel Davies, the inspector of the forces, and McNab, a former Defence Minister. The campaign was given further stimulus when the 1909 German Naval Scare swept the country. A scare fuelled by the realization that the German Navy threatened British sea supremacy. The Defence League seized the opportunity to call further meetings, and resolutions were engineered calling for the institution of universal military training as an absolute necessity for the safety of the country. In response to the campaign and the 1909 Imperial Conference, a new Defence Bill was presented to Parliament on 2 December 1909. In just under two weeks, the Bill was pushed through its three readings, its committee stages and signed into law. A law aimed at satisfying the demands of the press, public and Defence League. Demands which viewed the Voluntary System as inadequate but viewed conscription with abhorrence. The Bill introduced into New Zealand a Defence force modelled on the Swiss Militia. It provided for a compulsory part-time force where civilians would be given basic military training without the objectionable features of conscription. Implementation of the Act was, unlike its rush through Parliament, extremely slow. Its provisions, in fact, were postponed until after the visit of Field Marshall Viscount Kitchener who had

Moulding an Imperial Army.

The Imperial Army training.

been invited to visit New Zealand and make recommendations on its defence preparations. Under the new Act, a Territorial force was established to be administered under four Military Districts Auckland, Wellington, Canterbury and Otago. Each Military District was to have a Field Force based on modern establishments. Each was to have four Brigades of Mounted Rifles (12 Regiments), four Brigades of Infantry (16 Battalions), four Brigades of Field Artillery, two four gun battery ammunition columns, four Engineer Companies, four Field Ambulances, and eight supply column corps (4 Mounted and 4 Infantry). The scheme provided for 27,000 Territorials, between the ages of 18 and 19 to be available for training each year - 2,700 to pass into the reserves annually with another 38,000 cadets being trained. The manpower was divided into 'junior and cadets' from 12 to 14 years old, and 'senior cadets' from 14 to 18 years old. Males at 18 until 21 were then to join the 'General Training Section' before entering the 'Reserves' from 21 to 30.

Kitchener, after reviewing all of New Zealand's defence forces had few modifications to recommend to the proposed scheme. He believed a commandant should replace the Council of Defence, a quota system for districts be established, the General Training section should cater for 18 to 25 year olds and the Reserve should control those from 25 to 30.

In July 1910 an Amendment Bill to the Defence Act was put to Parliament to implement Kitchener's recommendations. This was followed in September by the announcement that Colonel Godley, with the temporary rank of Major-General, would take up the duties of commandant of New Zealand's defence forces in place of the Council of Defence.In 1911 Major General Sir Alexander Godley, General Officer Commanding, formed the New Zealand Staff Corps and the New Zealand Permanent Staff to meet the need for staff officers and instructors. In the same year arrangements were made to send up to 10 officer cadets annually to the newly-created Royal Military College at Duntroon in Australia.

At the same time the General Headquarters was expanded and a New Zealand Section of the Imperial General Staff was established. These bodies were tasked with writing plans for

Major General Godley.

mobilization and giving effect to Imperial co-operation in defence matters, in short, for the creation of a segment of an Imperial Army. The reforms were also important for the increase in efficiency achieved. As a result, when war broke out on 4 August 1914, New Zealand was in a position to offer the "mother country"' Britain, an expeditionary force.

Chapter Six:

THE FIRST WORLD WAR

Although the terms of the Defence Act 1909 specified that only volunteers could serve abroad, men offered themselves in sufficient numbers to fill the "Main Body" and to supply reinforcements for the next two years. During the war the Territorial system continued to function and each military district contributed troops.

Samoa

New Zealand's initial response at the outbreak of the war was rapid: at the request of the Imperial Government a force of 1413 men left New Zealand to occupy German Samoa. This was accomplished in an unopposed landing on 29 August 1914.

The Main Body

Meanwhile another expeditionary force, intended for France, was soon recruited. Drawn from the 25,000 members of the recently raised Territorial Force these volunteers came to be known as the 'Main Body'. This expeditionary force combined four battalions of infantry, four mounted rifle regiments, a field artillery brigade with ammunition column and other ancillary arms. It left New Zealand on 14 October 1914 under the command of Major General Godley. Sailing with him were 8,427 officers and men and 3,815 horses, the largest single body of troops ever to leave New Zealand.

Samoa: Landing at Apia.

Samoa: Raising the Union Jack..

New Zealand: On a route march through Upper Hutt..

New Zealand: Smoko during a route march..

Departure of New Zealand troops for Europe.

The main body along the Hutt Road prior to embarkation.

New Zealanders on board H.M.N.Z. Athenic.

ANZAC Landing.

The New Zealand contingent linked up with an even larger Australian force to travel to Europe. While their convoy was at sea, they were redirected to Egypt, where they arrived on 3 December 1915.

In Egypt the first combat engagement of the War for New Zealanders was to take place. They engaged the Turkish enemy in defence of the Suez Canal on 2 February 1915.

Gallipoli

On 25 April 1915 the New Zealanders (who, initially less the Mounted Rifle Brigades, had been combined as the Australian and New Zealand Army Corps - ANZAC) landed on the Gallipoli Peninsula, where for the next 8 months they fought alongside the Australians in a desperate campaign against the Turks. Elsewhere

ANZAC Cove — Gallipoli.

Gallipoli: Charging the Turk.

on the Peninsula, British and French forces were also storming Turkish positions.

Notwithstanding the fine effort on the part of the ANZACs, a stalemate was quickly reached. For the soldiers, trench warfare in conditions of physical hardship and extremes of climate became the norm. Worse, they found themselves confined to an extremely small area. Few of the ANZAC trench systems ever penetrated further than 2,000 metres from the shoreline.

One of the most inspiring actions ever performed by New Zealand soldiers took place on Gallipoli when they stormed the heights overlooking the ANZAC lines. On 8 August 1915, New Zealanders attacked a feature called Chunuk Bair, the strategic key to the Peninsula . The crest was gained but strong Turkish counter attacks led to three days of bitter fighting with the New Zealanders taking heavy casualties, causing their relief late on the 9th by troops of the British New Army, who in turn were forced to withdraw on the 10th.

An example of the heavy fighting that took place on the slopes of Chunuk Bair is to be found in the Wellington Battalion which led the assault at 4.30 a.m. on the morning of 8 August. They were relieved at about midnight by comparatively fresh units - the Otago Battalion and the Wellington Mounted rifles. To quote C. E. W. Bean, the official Australian War Historian:

> "Of the 760 of the Wellington Battalion who had captured the height that morning, there came out

Gallipoli: Advancing on the Enemy.

New Zealanders: Charge forward with fixed bayonets.

> only 70 unwounded or slightly wounded men. Throughout the day not one had dreamt of leaving his post. Their uniforms were torn, their knees broken. They had had no water since the morning: they could talk only in whispers: their eyes were sunken: their knees trembled: some broke down and cried like children".

The New Zealand Infantry and Mounted Rifle Brigades started the battle with 4,549 men. After two days of heavy fighting they were reduced to a strength of 2,678. The Official New Zealand War History records:

> "August 8 was a day of tragedy for New Zealand, but no day in our calendar shines with greater glory".

After eight months of this trench stalemate, the ANZACs were withdrawn from the Peninsula. A withdrawal when in contact with the enemy is one of the most difficult of all tactical manoeuvers, if it is to be achieved without sustaining heavy casualties. By the use of ruse and excellent planning 3,491 men of the Australian and New Zealand Division were withdrawn off the beaches on the night of 18/19 December 1915 and the remaining 3,000 on the following night.

The ruse worked and the entrenched Turks, in places as close as 10 metres away, had no inkling of the massive ANZAC withdrawal taking place to their front. It was a tribute to the planning staffs and the soldiers who had to execute this difficult manoeuver, that no casualties were suffered by the New Zealanders during the evacuation.

Chunuk Bair: Corporal Nuku and Private Thompson, New Zealand Territorial Soldiers at the Gallipoli Memorial Service, 25th April 1990.

Between April and December 1915, 11,600 New Zealanders served on Gallipoli: 2,721 died on active service whilst 4,752 were wounded.

Sinai-Palestine

Following the return of the New Zealanders from Gallipoli to Egypt, they were reorganised into an infantry division and a mounted rifle brigade.

The New Zealand Mounted Rifle Brigade, comprised of 147 officers and 2,897 other ranks, served as part of the Australian and New Zealand Mounted Division and was deployed in April 1916 to the Sinai Peninsula. The Brigade took part in the battles leading up to the fall of Jerusalem and onward to Amman and

Middle East: New Zealander arriving.

Middle East: Training for the charge.

Jordan: New Zealand Mounted Rifles cross the West Bank.

Jordan: New Zealanders view Turks that did not retreat in time.

Jaffa: Watering the horses at Wadi Hesi.

the surrender of the Turkish 4th Army in September 1918. Turkish resistance collapsed and an armistice was effected on 31 October 1918.

This comparatively small force showed great resource and endurance. In 1919 Field Marshall Sir Edmund Allenby wrote of the New Zealanders:

> "nothing daunted these intrepid fighters: to them nothing was impossible".

During the long campaign 17,723 New Zealanders served in Palestine: 640 died on active service and 1,146 were wounded.

The Western Front

From Egypt the New Zealand Division was ordered to France, where it arrived in April 1916. Both sides were stalemated and the New Zealanders quickly became accustomed to the rigors of European trench warfare.

Their first major action was in the closing stages of the Somme offensive in September 1916: in 23 days of fighting 1,560 New Zealanders were killed and 5,440 were wounded.

During 1917 the Division took part in the battles for Messines and Passchendaele, again taking heavy casualties. The winter of 1917-18 was spent in the Polygon Wood sector - these "quiet" winter months alone coast nearly 3,000 casualties.

With a steady stream of reinforcements arriving from New Zealand, the Division was able to maintain its four-battalion brigades (other allied divisions having three-battalion brigades) and it became the strongest division on the Western Front.

France: New Zealander using a captured machine gun.

France: Artillery in action.

France: The Runner with a message.

Stretcher bearers carry a man out off the Flanders mud.

One man sleeps while two remain alert.

New Zealanders at the German front line.

Belgium: New Zealand infantry prepare.

New Zealand Artillery enjoying a brew of cocoa.

France: Christmas 1917 for New Zealanders.

In March 1918, the Germans launched an offensive which created a dangerous gap between the British IV and V Corps and the capture of Amiens seemed certain. The New Zealanders were rushed to fill this gap and, in confused fighting with an enemy flushed with victory, gradually managed to gain the upper hand and the British front line was stabilised. For the next four months the Division held part of the line defending Amiens.

The Battle of Bapaume, the final British offensive, started in August 1918. One of the Division's finest actions was on 4 November 1918 when the 3rd (Rifles) Brigade stormed and captured the medieval fortress town of Le Quesnoy, using scaling ladders to climb the 60-foot ramparts - a success which, according to Lieutenant General Harper, Commander of IV Corps, "did much to decide the finish of the war" on 11 November 1918.

After the war Field Marshal Earl Haig who commanded the British Armies, wrote of the New Zealanders:

> "...no division in France built up for itself a finer reputation, whether for gallantry of its conduct in battle or for excellence of its behaviour out of the line".

On armistice day 1918, New Zealand had 58,129 troops in the field, while an additional 10,000 were under training in New Zealand. In total, the troops provided for foreign service by New Zealand during the War represented 10 percent of its 1914 population and 41 percent of the 1914 male population between the ages of 20 and 45.

Casualties

During the First World War, 100,444 troops left New Zealand for service with the expeditionary forces: of these, 16,697 lost their lives and 41,317 were wounded - a 58 percent casualty rate.

Lance Corporal David Lee killed in action in France.

"Killed in Action" said the cable,
That is all the tale they tell
Of the brave young lad who loved us
Of the lad we loved so well.

How the life was sped we know not,
What the last word, look or thought,
Only that he did his duty
Died as bravely as he fought.

Chapter Seven:

BETWEEN THE WARS

After World War I the Army, though held in high esteem, was affected by a rapid policy of retrenchment. The War had had a tremendous effect upon New Zealand. Economically the cost to the Nation had been high and the Government could only reduce its expenditure by cutting the Defence budget. In addition a strong anti-war feeling had grown within New Zealand; so many young New Zealander's had been killed. The Public hoped that the newly created League of Nations would solve the World's problems peacefully. None wanted another war on such a devastating scale.

The immediate effect of the budget cuts was a reduction in the size of the Army. The four Military districts were reduced to three commands (Northern, Central and Southern). The Permanent Forces were reduced to training cadres, and the number of Territorial force units was reduced. Compulsory Military Training (CMT) was suspended until 1921 and officer cadets were no longer sent to the Royal Military College Duntroon.

The release of Major-General Chaytor's Report of 1921-22, virtually sealed the fate of the Army. Chaytor, the General Officer Commanding the New Zealand Army made several far reaching proposals on the organisation and training of the Army. In essence, he advocated that a small but highly trained corps of officers and non-commissioned officers be maintained to carry out administration and training of Territorials and

Cadets. He also advocated that other permanent forces be reduced to only sufficient personnel to provide for the care and maintenance of Defence works, war material and stores. The Territorial Force should consist of one Division and three Mounted Rifle Brigades, Heavy and Anti-Aircraft Batteries. The Force was to be equally divided into three commands, each sub-divided into four regimental districts.

Between 1921 and 1925 there was no pay for those in the Territorial Force who attended camps, but in 1925 more funds were available and payment was restored and out of a strength of 20,000 a total of 17,300 attended training. Steps were then taken to strengthen the Staff Corps and the Permanent Staff whose ranks had been reduced after the War.

The revival, unfortunately, was to be brief. In 1930 the Government again decided to suspend compulsory military training on economic grounds, though politically there was a strong feeling in favour of world peace. 'Cobbes Bill', introduced by the then Minister of Defence, had the effect of reducing the Territorial Force strength from 17,000 to 3,000 overnight. In addition the permanent staff was again reduced, pay for Territorials discontinued, and many ordnance Corps personnel were transferred to the civilian staff. The Army sank in numbers, efficiency, equipment and in public esteem. An apathetic New Zealand public did not care for defence.

By 1930 the post World War I military decline was in full swing - there was a strong feeling for world peace throughout the Empire, due to Britain's Labour Government, who were scaling down military involvement in New Zealand's area of interest, specifically Singapore.

The Forbes Government realised the implications of total disarmament to New Zealand's security, and asked for a defence paper from the Committee of Imperial Defence. Additional finance was pledged to assist in maintaining the viability of the Singapore base during the difficult depression years. Both these moves showed the Conservative Government of the day was prepared to make a separate stand from the British Government if New Zealand's security was at risk.

Under canvas, Amberley.

Machine gun training, 1930, at Mt Somers.

A cadre system was formed late in 1930 and early the next year the Territorial Force was established on a voluntary basis with a ceiling of 10,000.The Imperial Defence paper was received the same year, which placed a priority on New Zealand being able to mount an Expeditionary Force at short notice to assist in the Empire's defence.

The Army reached an all time low in 1932 with only $312,622 being spent, approximately (0.52% of Government expenditure). Major General Sinclair-Burgess was aware of the Army's deficiencies and convinced the Government to move towards preparing the nation for war. There was a high turnover of personnel, but by the end of that year, Territorial Force numbers stood at 7,903.

By 1933 most of the Army's expenditure was being channeled into the Singapore base, and the threat of Japan loomed large in the minds of New Zealand's public. New Zealand's Prime Minister tasked the Committee of Imperial Defence to produce a 'war book' and stated he felt it unwise to continue in a defenceless state.The theme for defence still rested with an Expeditionary Force, against the desires of General Sinclair-Burgess who felt more emphasis should be placed on a permanent presence in Singapore.

The major problem in the Army at this time was a lack of expertise and command ability to meet the increasing responsibility. To this end officer cadets were again sent to the Royal Military College, Duntroon, Australia.

Later that year, Michael Joseph Savage's Labour Government took office. They too recognised that a defence problem existed and a threat was present, but with an attitude of suspicion treated Defence as a 'necessary evil'. Savage, however, reluctantly admitted that a defence build up was necessary in view of international tensions. Unit establishments were reduced and more completely filled.

The theme of collective security at the Imperial Conference of 1937 was pushed by New Zealand's Prime Minister. In August of the same year the Army was given its first policy guideline for some years. This guideline returned New Zealand's defence thinking back to the nineteenth century. It envisaged an army

Motorised infantry.

Infantry: 1st Canterbury Battalion 1937.

consisting of a small mechanised Field Force together with a garrison force to protect the main ports.

The Manchurian crisis and Japan's attacks on China in 1937 reinforced the image of Japan as a threat to New Zealand. A positive counter move was called for by Britain to place more troops in the South Pacific. Britain could not satisfy this requirement as this would have meant over stretching her Defence resources. As a result the New Zealand Council of Defence was formed and a large recruiting campaign launched. Naval, Army and Air Boards were formed with Service representatives under a civilian secretary acting for the Minister of Defence.

At this stage the Territorial Force was still undermanned and units were amalgamated in an attempt to form a force that would be viable in war. The Labour Government would not conscript and so had to appeal for volunteers.

The policy stated at the time was that all the wealth and services of the Nation would be placed at Defence's disposal if a war broke out. This was an indication in Labour's changing attitude, and a realization that the world climate was such that war was imminent.

In 1938, a significant event took place that served to underline the fact that New Zealand's Army was ill-prepared for war. Four senior Colonels, with long and distinguished careers published a manifesto protesting about the poor state of the Army. They published their statement to counter a claim made by the Minister of Defence, and the Chief of the General Staff, that the New Zealand Army was in a state of efficient readiness for combat. The event known as the 'Colonel's Revolt' was subsequently passed off as being politically motivated. However the action of the four senior officers; a public rebuke of their superiors, could not be taken lightly.

The Army of 510 Regular Force and 7,111 Territorial Force, soldiers was once again in the limelight. The Government was forced to give further resources for defence.When war was declared on 3 September 1939, those additional resources paid dividends. The despatch of an expeditionary force to fight Germany was a realistic capability. Indeed the nation expected it for the Government could devise no better means of serving

Training in the 1930's.

the country's long term strategic interests. As the Prime Minister so forcefully stated:

> "Both with gratitude for the past, and with confidence in the future, we arrange ourselves without fear beside Britain. Where she goes, we go, where she stands, we stand...."

Chapter Eight:

THE SECOND WORLD WAR: 1939-45

On 3 September 1939 Michael Joseph Savage formally announced New Zealand's declaration of war against Germany. It was a declaration announced simultaneously to that of Great Britain, 9.30p.m. New Zealand Standard Time. Even before the declaration of War, No. 1 Platoon, A Company of the New Zealand Regular Force had embarked aboard HMS Leander at Auckland on 30 August 1939. The platoon was bound for Fanning Island, a small landfall 5,600 kilometres north-east of New Zealand, where it was to guard the strategic Pacific Ocean cable station.

On 6 September, Cabinet authorised the mobilization of a 6,600 strong volunteer "Special Force" which became the nucleus of the 2nd New Zealand Expeditionary Force (2NZEF), a title officially adopted on 12 December 1939. Age limits for the force were set down as between 21 and 35 and those who joined were volunteering for service, within or beyond New Zealand, for the duration of the War and 12 months thereafter.

Enlistment for the force started on 12 September and by the end of the day 5,419 men had volunteered.

On 18 September, the Maori people petitioned the Government for the establishment of a Maori unit for active service: recruiting began for 28 (Maori) Battalion on 9 October and the unit served with distinction with the 2nd New Zealand Division in the Middle East and Italy.

The Middle East

Major General B. C. Freyberg, V.C., D.S.O., was appointed to command 2NZEF. He insisted on a "charter" which laid down his responsibilities to the New Zealand Government and which gave him considerable discretion in the administration and training of the force.

During the next nine months nearly 20,000 men embarked for overseas service in 2 NZEF. The First and Third Echelons landed in Egypt but the Second Echelon, on the high seas when Germany invaded France, was diverted to the United Kingdom and landed in Scotland on 16 June 1940.

Although some transport and signals elements took part in General Wavell's first Libyan campaign in December 1940, the 2nd New Zealand Division as a whole did not engage the enemy until the campaign in Greece in April 1941.

On 1 March 1941 the Germans had occupied Bulgaria and advanced towards the north-eastern border of Greece: in the meantime the Greek Army was fighting an exhausting campaign in Albania to the northwest against the Italians.

The 2nd Division was deployed to Greece during March, as part of an Allied force (W Force) to support the outnumbered and tired Greeks. The New Zealanders moved to north-eastern Greece by road and rail from Athens. Here 4 and 6 Brigades occupied a long 24-kilometre right flank sector of the Aliakmon Line south of the Aliakmon River: 5 Brigade holding a depth position about 16 kilometres to the south, near Mount Olympus.

On 6 April the Germans invaded Yugoslavia and Greece, immediately threatening to outflank the New Zealanders to the west. Two days later the New Zealanders were forced to start a withdrawal south, through the 5 Brigade position.

The New Zealanders continued to execute an excellent fighting withdrawal for 320 kilometres down the eastern seaboard of the Greek mainland, delaying the Germans, all the way. Between 24-27 April, 4 and 5 Brigades were evacuated by the Navy from a port south-east of Athens and taken to Crete: 6 Brigade was evacuated from beaches south of Sparta on 28 and 29 April, being taken directly back to Alexandria in Egypt.

New Zealand: Recruits march bound for Papakura Camp.

New Zealand troops arriving in Piraeus.

New Zealand 25 pounder in Olympus Pass.

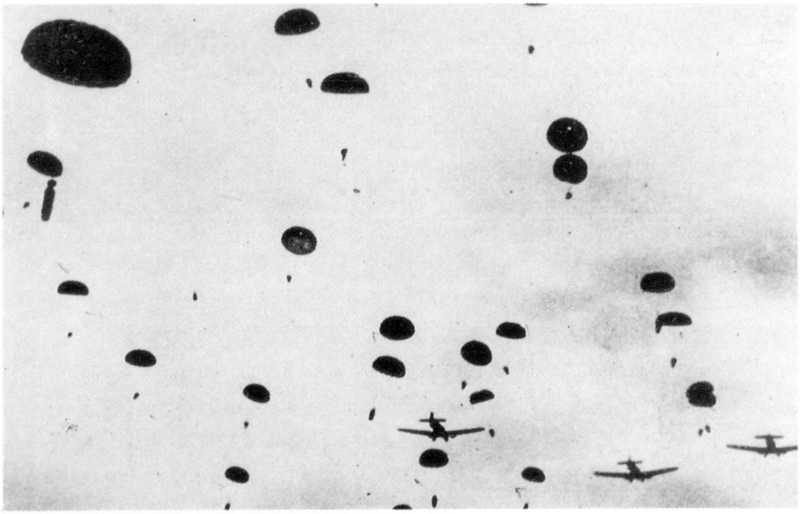

Crete: German parachute descent.
(Photo courtesy of Historical Publications Branch, Department of Internal Affairs)

Crete: Exhausted New Zealanders in retreat.

General Freyberg was evacuated to Crete on 28 April - he had "disregarded" an order for him to leave Greece on 23 April. On 30 April he was appointed to command all British, Australian, and New Zealand troops on Crete - a total of about 28,600 men - most of whom were evacuees from Greece. Crete was to be defended as a strategic naval base in the eastern Mediterranean.

Scant time was provided to prepare the island for defence and on 20 May the Germans launched an airborne assault on Crete from airfields on the Greek mainland. Within ten days the Germans had taken Crete and over 13,000 men of Freyberg's command were dead or taken prisoner.

The New Zealanders, on the north-western edge of the island, had taken much of the initial brunt of the German attack and had been forced to withdraw, this time over the rugged central mountain spine of Crete, to the port of Sfaika in the south. Again the Royal Navy, against heavy odds, managed to evacuate thousands of weary soldiers back to Egypt.

The exhausted 2nd New Zealand Division regrouped in Egypt where its losses in Greece and Crete were replenished by reinforcements from New Zealand.

Acknowledged as a hazardous operation from the very start, the two months of April and May 1941 resulted in the deaths of 932 New Zealanders, 1,354 were wounded and evacuated and 4,036 were taken prisoner by the Germans: of the POW's, 730 had been wounded before capture. These casualty figures were second only to the appalling casualties suffered in 23 days on the Somme 25 years earlier.

By November 1941 the 2nd Division was again in action: this time as part of the 8th Army's second Libyan campaign in Cyrenaica to the west of Egypt. The aim was to entrap the German Afrika Corps. The Germans were however not trapped, nevertheless they were forced to withdraw to El Aghelia. The Division suffered heavy casualties and was withdrawn from battle in December 1941.

There were growing fears at this time that the German invasion of Russia with a swing south through the Caucasus mountains, could result in a direct threat to Turkey and Syria.

Middle East: Capturing the enemy.

Middle East: Advance under gunfire.

Libya: Anti-tank Regiment in desert formation.

Libya: Maori patrol in Bardia.

Tobruk: Advancing on the enemy.

Middle East: Long range desert group.

Between February and June 1942, the Division was attached to the British 9th Army and occupied position in northern Syria. During this deployment, the New Zealanders became very aware of the actions of pro-Axis fifth column elements in Syria and the Syrians' dislike of French rule which, aside from that of Vicy France, the British were supporting.

A German advance in the Desert, the capture of Tobruk and an imminent threat of an Axis breakthrough to the Suez Canal, necessitated the speedy return of the 2nd Division to the 8th Army at Minqar Qaim on Egypt's western desert frontier. The move, over a distance of 1,500 kilometres, was achieved in a week.

Within days of the redeployment of the New Zealanders, the 8th Army was forced to withdraw. The 2nd Division at Minqar Qaim found itself surrounded by advancing German Panzer forces. Rather than surrender or accept capture, the Division executed a successful breakout and a fighting withdrawal from the encirclement on the night of 27-28 June. The division moved back to the Alamein Line, 160 kilometres west of Cairo. Despite heavy fighting during the ensuing months, the Alamein Line held fast.

On 23 October 1942, the 8th Army under the leadership of its new commander, General Montgomery, attacked the Germans at El Alamein. This successful attack was the start of an advance which rolled the Axis forces westwards across the desert and terminated in their surrender in Tunisia on 13 May 1943.

Italy

With the defeat of the German Afrika corps the New Zealanders were redeployed for service in Italy. In September 1943, the Division landed in Europe to fight a completely different kind of battle. Over the next 18 months it took part in severe fighting all the way up the Italian peninsula. Crossing of the Sangro River, the battle for Cassino in May 1944, the occupation of Rome on 4 June, of Florence on 4 August, action on the Gothic Line, action on the Adriatic coast and finally the advance to Trieste (occupied on 9 April 1945) are to name but the most notable actions the

Tunisia: Signpost on the way to Enfidaville.

Tunisia: New Zealand Mule Pack Company.

division was involved in. On 2 May 1945 German forces in Italy, after fighting a fierce rearguard finally surrendered.

Throughout its campaigning the soldiers of the Division had acquitted themselves well. The German 14 Panzer Corps post-operation report after Cassino stated that:

> "The New Zealand soldier is physically fit and strong. He is well-trained and formidable in close-range fighting and steadier than an Englishman. He does not shrink from hand-to-hand fighting. In many cases strong points had to be wiped out to the last man, as they refused to surrender".

Italy: Crossing the Sangro River.

Italy: The day Cassino fell.

At the peak of its strength in February 1945 there were 34,953 New Zealanders serving with 2 NZEF in Europe. Between 1940 and 1945, 6,068 died whilst on active service and 15,108 were wounded: 8,369 men were taken prisoner, of whom 513 died whilst in captivity.

The Pacific:

On 1 November 1940, the New Zealand Army's 8 Brigade landed in Fiji. It was the first time that a Crown Colony had been garrisoned by troops from one of the self-governing Dominions.

New Zealand formally declared war against Japan at 11 a.m. New Zealand Summer Time on 8 December 1941. A second

Italy: Over the top at Faenza.

Italy: Snowed up at sogna.

Italy: 18 Battalion crossing the Po.

brigade, 14 Brigade, was raised in New Zealand the following month. It was shipped to Fiji, where the combined brigades were given divisional status and officially titled B-Force 2NZEF.

On 14 May 1942, B-Force was retitled the 3rd New Zealand Division and during June and July returned to New Zealand after being relieved by the US Army's 37th Division.

Back home the Division was reorganised and trained in jungle warfare. Major General H. E. Barrowclough was appointed General Officer Commanding 2NZEF in the Pacific (2NZEF IP) and the Division deployed by sea to New Caledonia in late 1942 and early 1943.

During this period New Zealand army detachments were stationed on Norfolk Island (N-Force) and Tonga (T-Force).

In August 1943, the 3rd New Zealand Division was deployed to an advanced base on Guadalcanal in the Solomon Islands. A month later 14 Brigade landed on Vella Lavella and on 27 October 8 Brigade made a successful landing on islands in the Treasury Group. The ensuing operations to clear the islands of Japanese, resulted in fighting in appalling climatic and physical conditions. Vella Lavella was declared secure on 9 October and organised resistance by Japanese in the Treasury Islands ceased on 12 November 1943.

A 300-strong raiding party, most of whom were from 30 Battalion, made a night landing on Nissan Island in the Green Islands group on 30 January 1944. After reconnoitering for 24 hours, the group was withdrawn by sea. This was in preparation for a full-scale amphibious landing by the 3rd New Zealand Division (less 8 Brigade) and United States troops on 15 February. Organised Japanese resistance ceased on 20 February but mop–ping up operations continued until the end of the month.

Over the next few months the strength of the Division was depleted to provide reinforcements for the 2nd New Zealand Division in Italy and for the provision of manpower for essential industries in New Zealand.

The 3rd New Zealand Division was officially disbanded on 20 October 1944. On 14 August 1945 Japan unconditionally accepted the Allied surrender terms.

Pacific: Beach landing.

Pacific: Fighting the conditions.

At the peak of its strength in December 1943, there were 17,891 New Zealanders serving in 2NZEF IP. Two Hundred and three men of the 3rd New Zealand Division died whilst on active service and 213 were wounded: 26 men were taken prisoner of whom 19 died in captivity.

Casualties:

A total of 104,988 men and women served overseas with 2 NZEF during the Second World War: 6,839 died on active service and 16,543 were wounded.

New Zealand - the Home Front

The National Military Reserve was established in May 1939. In order to augment the Territorial Forces. Because of the number of volunteer units forming throughout the country, the War Cabinet approved of the establishment of a Home Guard in August 1940.

The object of the Guard was defined as being to "augment local defences by providing for static defence of localities, the protection of vulnerable and key points and to give timely notice of enemy movements to superior military authorities".

Limited in equipment and wearing armbands for identification, the Home Guard carried out valuable work in building tank traps and defensive works at the more vulnerable beaches.

The Army took control of the Home Guard in August 1941 and appointed former General Officer Commanding New Zealand Forces, Brigadier R. Young, as Director General.

From this time commissions were granted and by the end of 1942 all Homeguardsmen had been issued with battle dress and boots. The country was divided into 33 zones, each zone having a Regular Commander for the Territorial and Home Guard units. Tommy guns, machine guns, and rifles were issued in quantity.

After Japan's entry into the war, registration for the Home Guard was made compulsory for men of military age not already in the army and for men aged between 46 and 50. In December 1943, the war situation had improved sufficiently for the Home Guard to be placed on the Reserve. At the height of its strength in March 1943, the Home Guard numbered 124,194 men.

Home Guard: Otorohanga

Chapter Nine:

THE KOREAN WAR

The Korean War which began on 25 June 1950, was the result of the power vacuum caused by the defeat of Japan in 1945 together with the Cold War rivalry between the United States and Russia. After Japan's defeat the United States and the Russians agreed that the Soviets would accept the surrender of the Japanese troops in Korea north of the 38 Parallel and the Americans would accept the surrender of all those to the south.

As post-war relations between the United States and Russia continued to deteriorate the 38 Parallel began to take on the appearance of a frontier. The United States put the issue before the United Nations in 1947 and a UN Temporary Commission on Korea was set up to supervise elections which were to be held before 31 March 1948. The Russians refused the Commission access to the North and therefore the Commission was only able to supervise the Southern elections.

The situation erupted into conflict when North Korea invaded the South. The United Nations condemned the invasion and ordered the North to cease hostilities and withdraw. When this order was ignored, a resolution was passed in the United Nations asking all members to give South Korea as much assistance as required to resist the attack.

The New Zealand Government's initial response to the call from the United Nations was to despatch two frigates to serve in Korean waters. However the continued deterioration in the sit–

uation made the provision of ground forces crucial. The Chief of General Staff, Major General K. L. Steward, initially opposed the commitment of ground forces from New Zealand as they would be too small to be self-sufficient. The Regular Force in 1950 numbered only 3,500 and the introduction of Compulsory Military Training in 1949 had over-stretched the Army's resources. Ignoring Major-General Stewart's opposition, the New Zealand government announced on 26 July 1950 that it would provide one artillery regiment for service with the United Nations ground force.

New Zealand's original force comprised Headquarters Kayforce, 16th Field Regiment RNZA, a signals troop, a light aid detachment, a transport platoon, and a small reinforcement training unit, the total strength being 70 officers and 974 other ranks.

Korea: Kiwi Hill, H.Q. 16th Field Regiment.

Korea: Fighting General Winter.

Korea: The New Zealand Concert Party.

The force arrived in Pusan, Korea by sea on New Year's Eve 1950, and was attached to the 27th British Brigade.

The 16th Field Regiment first went into action on 29 January 1951 and remained on active service for the next two and a half years. The Regiment's most famous battle was Kapyong in support of the 3rd Battalion, Royal Australian Regiment, fought during April 1951. In July 1951 the land contingents from the various commonwealth nations amalgamated to form the Commonwealth Division.

After the signing of the armistice in July 1954, reductions to Kayforce's strength were gradually made. The 16th Field Regiment which had fired over three-quarters of a million shells during the war, and other corps' elements were withdrawn in 1955. Residual members of the force were concentrated into the 10th Transport Company RNZASC. The last elements of Kayforce returned to New Zealand in 1957.

Casualties:

A total of 3,794 soldiers served in Kayforce during the Korean War: 33 died on active service, 79 were wounded and 1 was taken prisoner by the North Koreans.

Korea: Contact with the locals.

Chapter Ten:
MALAYAN CAMPAIGN

When Japanese resistance collapsed in Malaya at the end of the Burma campaign, a number of its troops were still in the jungle. The task of dealing with the Japanese remnant was given to the predominantly Chinese Malay guerilla army raised by Colonel Spencer Chapman. Though an effective fighting force, this guerilla army was distrusted by the Malays who were suspicious of its communist leanings. Many believed that its aim was to impose Chinese control over the country.

Once the guerilla army had completed its task of rounding up remnants of the Japanese army, it commenced a campaign of terror. Persuaded by their communist mentors to turn against the British, the leaders of the guerilla army conducted terrorist operations from their jungle bases. In response a State of Emergency was declared in June 1948 that was to last until July 1960.

British troops were sent to destroy the guerrillas, now titled Communist Terrorists, and New Zealand was asked to assist. In late 1955 a squadron of the Special Air Service (SAS) was raised in New Zealand for service in Malaya. Consisting of six officers and 127 other ranks, it was flown to Malaya to become part of the British Far East Strategic Reserve. Early in 1956, having completed parachute training in Singapore, the Squadron was attached to the British 22nd SAS Regiment which was in action against communist terrorists in Malaya.

Malaya: SAS on operations.

The Squadron spent two years on active service in Malaya, during which time its members spent an average of 17 months on jungle operations. Returning to New Zealand in late 1957, the Squadron was replaced on active service by the 1st Battalion, the New Zealand Regiment which had a strength of 38 officers and 702 other ranks.

Towards the end of 1959, the 1st Battalion was itself replaced by the 2nd Battalion, the New Zealand Regiment which conducted operations against terrorists along the Malay-Thai border.

New Zealand's infantry presence however, was retained in Malaysia. As part of a reorganisation in 1964, the 1st and 2nd Battalions of the New Zealand Regiment were amalgamated to form the 1st Battalion, Royal New Zealand Infantry Regiment

SAS troopers parachute training for Malaya service.

which was based in Malacca, Malaysia. In 1969 the Battalion was deployed to Singapore where it remained until 1989 when it returned to New Zealand.

Confrontation:

The newly-formed 1st Battalion, Royal New Zealand Infantry Regiment was first employed on active service in Malaysia, as part of the 28th Commonwealth Infantry Brigade Group, during the period of "Confrontation" between Malaysia and Indonesia from August 1964 until August 1966.

The Battalion was also sent on active service to Borneo on two separate occasions. Between May and October 1965 the Battalion, under the command of Lieutenant Colonel R. M. Gurr, was attached to the 19th British Infantry Brigade Group: between May and September 1966 the Battalion, under the command of Lieutenant Colonel B. M. Poananga, was attached to the 99th Gurkha Infantry Brigade Group. Soldiers from the latter Battalion were often referred to as the "big Gurkhas"' due to the number of Maoris in the unit and the Battalion's overall competence in jungle warfare.

Between February 1965 and November 1966, four separate New Zealand SAS detachments were deployed from New Zealand and served in Borneo under the operational command of the British 22nd SAS Regiment. The first detachment was based in Kughing, with subsequent detachments being based on the island of Labuan. Their tasks included reconnaissance and ambush missions.

Casualties

Seven New Zealand soldiers died in action during the Malayan Emergency and seven were wounded. In addition two soldiers died during the confrontation and two were wounded.

Malaya: On patrol.

Malaya: Taking a break.

SPECIAL ORDER OF THE DAY : 1 NZ SAS

To Major Velvin and All Ranks of 1 NZ SAS:

Your unit has been specially selected to represent the New Zealand Army in the discharge of our treaty obligations to Thailand, in association with forces from the United States, Australia and other member nations of SEATO. I know that you can be counted upon to discharge your duties in such a way as to reflect credit on this country and upon your Service.

This task will be an onerous one; it will call for the maintenance of a high standard of personal discipline and the exercise of all the determination for which the SAS is noted. You will be entering Thailand during a climatic period which will test your physical stamina. You must expect your living conditions to be hard and your training schedule arduous. At the same time this deployment provides you with an excellent opportunity to obtain further first-hand experience of the terrain, the climate and the peoples of South East Asia.

Remember that you will be entering a country which prides itself upon its independence and the freedom of its citizens. Remember in all your dealings with Thai nationals, of whatever degree, that you are there as a welcome guest in their country - but still as a guest. You must show every cooperation and understanding in your contacts with the members of the Royal Thai Armed Forces and the forces of our Allied partners.

The best of good fortune to you all in this important mission.

Army Headquarters,
WELLINGTON.
26 May 1962

Major General
CHIEF OF THE GENERAL STAFF

Thailand: Committing the SAS.

Chapter Eleven:

THE VIETNAM WAR

In the nineteenth century France had taken control of Vietnam and made it an integral part of its Indo-Chinese Empire. During the Second World War Vietnam had fallen to Japan and as in Malaya, guerilla forces were raised to fight the occupiers. Eventually Vietnam was liberated by the forces of Britain and China. Britain took control of the South, while Chinese forces occupied the north. At the end of the war France decided to reoccupy its former territory. When its forces returned in early 1946 they discovered that the North was already controlled by the Viet Minh, Vietnam's communists. Unsuccessful in their attempts to negotiate an agreement, the French and Viet Minh forces were at war within a year. The Viet Minh established the Democratic Republic of Vietnam in the North, which was immediately recognised by the Soviet Union of the Peoples Republic of China.

For the next eight years France struggled to impose its will in a ruthless guerilla war. After the defeat at Dien Bien Phu in 1954, the French decided to withdraw from Indo-China. Vietnam was partitioned at the 17th Parallel with the Viet Minh controlling their Democratic Republic of Vietnam to the North. To the South a non-communist Republic of Vietnam was established. Unlike its northern counterpart the government of the Southern republic had difficulty controlling its territory. In particular, the Com–

munist National Liberation Front, with its military arm the Viet Cong, were a destabilising influence. The United States viewing the Viet Cong as disguised Northern aggression decided to assist the Southern State with military forces. At the same time they sought similar assistance from their allies.

New Zealand's response was carefully considered and initially consisted of a detachment of Royal New Zealand Engineers. Consisting of two officers and 20 other ranks this contingent was despatched in June 1964. They were sent to the Southern Republic in a non-combatant capacity to undertake reconstruction tasks in and around the town of Thu Do Mot. At the same time a small administrative headquarters was established in Saigon.

On 27 May 1965 the Prime Minister, Sir Keith Holyoake, announced the Government's decision to send 161 Battery, Royal New Zealand Artillery to South Vietnam in a combat role. The Engineers were replaced by the Battery in July 1965. Comprised of nine officers and 101 other ranks, 161 Battery was initially under command of the United States Army's 173rd Airborne Brigade based at Bien Hoa near Saigon.

In June 1966 the Battery was reassigned to the 1st Australian Task Force at Nui Dat, in Phuoc Tuy Province east of Saigon. From then until its withdrawal in May 1971, the Battery served with Royal Australian Artillery field regiments in support of Australian and New Zealand infantry units.

In May 1967, New Zealand's combat strength in Vietnam was increased by a 182-strong rifle company, designated Victor One Company, from the 1st Battalion Royal New Zealand Infantry Regiment in Malaysia. In December 1967 Victor One Company was joined by Whisky One Company, also from the 1st Battalion. Both companies came under the Australian Task Force's command and formed part of an ANZAC infantry battalion.

The rifle companies were deployed on infantry operations in Phuoc Tuy Province and were replaced several times, usually after a 12-month tour of duty. Whiskey Three Company was withdrawn without replacement in November 1970 and Victor Six Company was withdrawn without replacement in December 1971.

Vietnam: Fire mission.

Vietnam: Infantry being carried on patrol.

New Zealand's military presence in South Vietnam was also increased in May 1967 with the arrival of the New Zealand Services' Medical Team, a 19-strong tri-service detachment. The New Zealanders, provided under the Military Public Health Programme, relieved a United States Army medical team at Bong Son in Binh Dinh Province. They dispensed medical care to the local civilian community in the main, but also treated military casualties who were brought into the Bon Son Dispensary - including South Vietnamese Army personnel and Viet Cong prisoners.

In June 1969 the team moved from the old dispensary into the new 100-bed Bong Son Impact Hospital. The average bed-state was 92 and approximately 46,000 outpatients (mostly civilians) were treated annually before the team's withdrawal in December 1971.

In November 1968, New Zealand's contribution to the 1st Australian Task Force was increased by the deployment of 4 Troop, New Zealand Special Air Service, comprising an officer and 25 other ranks. The Troop was attached to an Australian SAS Squadron at Nui Dat and carried out long-range reconnaissance and the ambushing of enemy supply routes until being withdrawn in February 1971.

In October 1970 the 1st New Zealand Army Training Team Vietnam, comprising 25 advisers, arrived in Vietnam and established a National Training centre for South Vietnamese Regional Force soldiers at Chi Lang, west of Saigon near the Cambodian border. The Centre trained about 8,000 platoon commanders and junior leaders annually - in the use of small arms and minor tactics.

February 1972 saw the arrival in Vietnam of the 2nd New Zealand Army Training Team Vietnam, dispatched to assist a United States Army Training Team with the training of Cambodian infantry battalions. Eighteen advisers were stationed with the Americans at Dong Ba Thin near Cam Rhan Bay about 320 kilometres north of Saigon. Apart from military training, the Team provided first aid instruction and specialist medical instruction at Dong Ba Thin's 50-bed hospital.

Vietnam: River crossing.

The last of the New Zealand Army's combat elements were withdrawn from South Vietnam in December 1971: the two training teams and the New Zealand headquarters in Saigon were withdrawn by the newly-elected Labour Government in December 1972.

At the highest peak, in November 1968, New Zealanders in South Vietnam numbered 543: a total of 3,890 troops (all volunteers) served in Vietnam between June 1964 and December 1972.

Casualties:

Thirty-five New Zealanders were killed in action and 187 were wounded.

Vietnam: Taking a break.

Vietnam: New Zealanders with Vietcong.

Vietnam: 161 Battery position.

Chapter Twelve:

POST-WAR DEVELOPMENTS

After the war 2 NZEF and home service units were progressively demobilised and only a small permanent force, with an established strength of 3,747 was retained.

In 1948 the New Zealand Staff Corps, the New Zealand Permanent Staff and the New Zealand Permanent Army Service Corps were disbanded and replaced with 17 functional Corps.

Post-war troubles in Palestine and the Middle East had a profound effect on New Zealand's defence posture as apart from the strategic importance of the Suez Canal, there was a traditional interest resulting from the commitment of New Zealand troops to the area during the two World Wars.

It was assumed at the time that the Middle East would remain as New Zealand's major area of assistance towards Commonwealth defence - an assumption that was to change in the early to mid-1950's when South East Asia became New Zealand's primary area of strategic interest.

In 1949 it was decided to raise a division for service in the Middle East, should the need arise, and the Government promptly decided on steps to train sufficient men to fulfill this commitment.

A national referendum was held on 3 August 1949 on the issue of conscription for territorial service; 553,016 votes were cast in favour of conscription, with 152,443 against.

The results were described by the Labour Prime Minister, Mr Fraser, as being indicative of the people of New Zealand to "stand shoulder to shoulder with the people of the British Commonwealth for democratic freedom".

The Army Act 1950 superseded the Defence Act 1909 and resulted in the combination of the regular and territorial forces to form "The New Zealand Army", the first time the title had been officially used.

Compulsory Military Training

The Army now comprised an infantry division, an armoured brigade, and a medium regiment of artillery, as well as coastal and anti-aircraft artillery units and static support units. The bulk of the manning was by territorial force soldiers trained under the Compulsory Military Training (CMT) scheme for which the Government had been given a clear mandate by the 1949 referendum.

All young men, on reaching the age of 18, were required to register with the Department of Labour and Employment. Apart from those exempted for medical or compassionate reasons, all had to undergo 14 weeks' full-time training, after which they were posted to a territorial unit for three years.

In their units, territorials had to complete 20 days' training each year, including a 14-day annual camp. After three years' service, the territorial soldier was allowed to transfer to the Reserve, if he wished, for a six-year period during which he was not required to complete any further training.

The first CMT Intake marched in for training on 9 May 1950. A total of 63,033 men were trained under the CMT scheme before it was abolished by the Labour Government in early 1958, at which time territorial service became voluntary.

The Labour Government under Nash decided to concentrate defence spending on a Regular Force cadre, and a volunteer Territorial Army. A Government Defence White Paper published in 1958, proposed a reorganisation of the army. These proposals were to be implemented on 1 April 1959. The Regular Force was divided into two sections. The first was a static section responsible for training and logistics. The second segment comprised an operational Brigade Group, for overseas commitment, which included within its structure, the battalion deployed in Malaya.

Compulsory military training.

The changes implemented by Nash's cabinet lasted a little over four years. In 1960 National, under Keith Holyoake, was once more on the treasury benches. This second National Government reintroduced compulsory military training in 1962, though this time it was called National Service. Under the provisions of the National Service Act all males were required to register on their 20th birthday with the Department of Labour. Ballots were then conducted to decide who would undertake compulsory service. Those selected were required to complete three months' initial full-time training, followed by an annual commitment of three weeks part-time training. The first National Service intake marched in for training on 10 March 1962.

While National service was filling the ranks of the Territorial Force, deeper changes were taking place in the country's defence organisation. Holyoake's Cabinet agreed in 1962 to the establishment of a new Department of Defence. This Department was to advise the Minister on policy, planning, and expenditure. The new department was formally established on 1 January 1964. On its formation, a civil servant became departmental head and adviser to the Minister.

The formation and establishment of the Defence Department was paralleled by a reorganisation of the army. This reorganisation was necessary to meet the commitment undertaken by the Government in joining the South-East Asian Treaty Organisation (SEATO). National Service, which was to last until 1972, was specifically designed to furnish additional manpower for deployment of a brigade sized formation in South-East Asia, if required. To meet the need the army was organised into a Combat Brigade and a Logistics Supply Group. The Combat Brigade Group, consisted of 3,250 Regular Force and 10,000 Territorial Force soldiers. The Logistics Supply Group, organised to administer, train, and equip the combat field force, was a smaller formation consisting of 3,000 soldiers.

In 1972, Norman Kirk headed the newly elected third Labour Government ended compulsory national service. The Territorials were once again to be volunteers, a change not altered when the Muldoon National Government swept back to power in 1975.

National did, however, once again examine the nation's defences. Another Defence Review was issued in 1978, followed in 1979 by another reorganisation of the army. The Command structure was abolished and replaced by a Land Force and Task Force regional headquarters.

Five years later in 1983 another Defence Review was issued. Under it, a Ready Reaction Force was established, comprising of a deployable battalion group of approximately 1,200 Regular Force soldiers. The 1983 review also committed the army to maintaining the Special Air Service (SAS) squadron in a state of readiness against possible terrorist attacks.

Under the fourth Labour government the army, like the rest of society, has had to face rapid change. The old alliances have

Exercising armour and anti-aircraft in the 1950's.

Training in the 1970's: An integrated army.

been challenged and internal administration radically altered. In 1986 defence was re-examined by the Corner committee and in 1989 a resource management review was undertaken by Derek Quigley. In response to these reviews, the Ministry of Defence was radically altered with the Defence Fores and the Civilian Ministry being split. New Zealand Defence Forces are to concern themselves with operational matters while the Ministry reviews policy. Yet the primary task given to today's army is the same as it always has been. It is to preserve the security and integrity of New Zealand. To achieve this it has been directed to help pro–mote security and stability in the South Pacific by being able to respond militarily to low level emergencies.

National Service Soldiers — Waiouru.

Training above the trees — Waiouru.

Chapter Thirteen:
PEACEKEEPING

Since its inception at the end of World War II, New Zealand has strongly supported the United Nations. An important part of New Zealand's support has been continuing contributions to its peacekeeping activities. In all, the New Zealand Army has been involved in eleven United Nations peacekeeping operations. In addition, New Zealand has participated in two non-United Nations peacekeeping initiatives: the Commonwealth Monitoring Force in Rhodesia and the Multinational Force and Observers in the Sinai.

New Zealand first became directly involved in peacekeeping in 1951 when the Government responded positively to a request from the Secretary-General of the United Nations for three military observers to serve with the United Nations Military Observer Group in India and Pakistan (UNMOGIP).

In 1976 New Zealand withdrew from UNMOGIP for reasons of economy. In addition to UNMOGIP the New Zealand Army has contributed, since 1954, officers to the United Nations Truce Supervision Organization (UNTSO) established in 1948. UNTSO was established to supervise the four armistice agreements between Israel and its neighbours: Egypt, Jordan, Syria and the Lebanon. Its task has been to report on compliance (and lack of compliance) with the armistice agreements of 1949 and later the cease-fire arrangements after the Suez War in 1956, the Six-Day War of 1967 and the Yom Kippur War of 1973. UNTSO personnel are based at six main locations: East Jerusalem (HQ), Nahariya (Northern Israel), Tiberius (NE Israel), Damascus, Cairo and Gaza.

One New Zealand officer was detached from UNTSO in 1956 to serve with the United Nations Emergency Force I (UNEFI). The UNEFI was established to secure and supervise the withdrawal of British, French and Israeli forces after their attack on Egypt in 1956; thereafter it served as a buffer between Egypt and Israel along the armistice line, at the Gaza Strip and at Sharm-el-Sheikh. It operated successfully until May 1967 when it was required to withdraw by Egypt - in whose territory it was located - immediately prior to the outbreak of hostilities between Egypt and Israel (the 'Six Day War').

In 1958 another New Zealand officer was detached from UNTSO to serve with the United Nations Observation Group in Lebanon (UNOGIL). Lebanon was gripped by civil strife in mid-1958, and as part of efforts to resolve the situation UNOGIL was established to ensure that arms and personnel were not being illegally infiltrated into the country.

A further two New Zealand officers were detached from UNTSO from 1960-61 to serve with the United Nations Operation in the Congo (ONUC). The ONUC was initially established to ensure that Belgian forces were withdrawn following the granting of independence to the Congo (Zaire) in June 1960, to assist the new government in maintaining law and order and to provide technical assistance. It was also given the tasks of preventing the recurrence of civil war, and of removing mercenaries and all other foreign military personnel not under UN command. Following the attempted secession by Katanga province in 1961, ONUC was given the further task of maintaining Zaire's territorial integrity.

Two years after ONUC, New Zealand had one officer detached from UNTSO to serve with the United Nations Yemen Observation Mission (UNYOM). UNYOM was established under the auspices of UNTSO to observe the implementation of the disengagement agreement between Saudi Arabia and the then United Arab Republic, (Egypt), who had become embroiled in Yemen's civil war. The United Nations mission was withdrawn

South Lebanon 1979: New Zealanders with PLO.

Sinai: Major Tymkin checking water equipment.

at the request of these two countries, having largely failed to achieve its objectives due to the intractability of the conflict and inadequate resources.

In 1973 the United Nations Emergency Force II (UNEF II) was established to supervise the cease-fire and redeployment of forces in the Sinai following the Egypt-Israeli armistice in 1973. It also manned and controlled buffer zones set up under agreements in 1974 and 1975. When initially deployed, UNEF II had posted to its strength, New Zealand military observers detached from UNTSO.

A year after UNEF II was deployed, New Zealand Military observers were attached to the United Nations Disengagement Force (UNDOF) from UNTSO. UNDOF was created in June 1974 to supervise the separation of Israeli and Syrian forces in the Golan Heights region of Syria.

Four years after UNDOF New Zealand officers serving with UNTSO were posted to serve with the United Nations Interim Force in Lebanon (UNIFIL).

Following Israel's invasion of the Lebanon, UNIFIL was established in March 1978 to monitor Israeli withdrawal from southern Lebanon, to restore peace and security and to assist in establishing political authority in the territory. Given the internal divisions in Lebanon as well as outside involvement, UNIFIL has made little progress with these objectives. It could do nothing to prevent a further invasion of Lebanon by Israel in June 1982 but has remained in existence following Israeli withdrawal.

With the cessation of hostilities between Iran and Iraq in 1988 the United Nations Iran Iraq Military Observer Group (UNIMOG) was formed. UNIMOG was established to observe the cease-fire line between Iran and Iraq and to monitor all troop withdrawals. Operating on both sides of the border it has dual headquarters in Teheran and Baghdad.New Zealand Army officers were posted to UNIMOG in August 1989.

A year later the United Nations Transition Assistance Group (UNTAG) was established to supervise the withdrawal of South African forces from Namibia and to assist in Namibia's transition to independence, including supervision of elections.

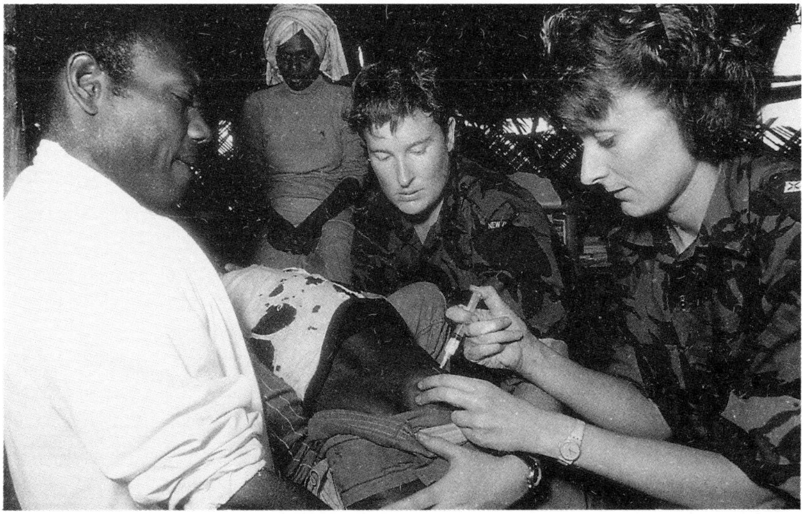

Vanuatu: Innoculation programme 1984.

Namibia: Guard duty at night 1990.

A 14 man New Zealand Army engineer team and a 32 strong contingent of New Zealand police served with UNTAG.

In addition to the formal United Nations Forces the New Zealand Army has had five engineers attached to the United Nations Afghanistan Co-ordination Office in Pakistan. This detachment teaches mine awareness and mine clearing techniques to Afghan refugees. The United Nations de-mining programme is not, strictly speaking, a peacekeeping operation, but is notable for its use of military personnel in a humanitarian role.The 5th N.Z. Mine Clearance Training team left on February 24, 1991.

Casualties:

Two New Zealand officers have been wounded while serving with the United Nations Forces.

Commonwealth Cease-Fire Monitoring Force (CMF): 1979-80

The CMF was established by the Commonwealth following the Lancaster House Agreement whereby Rhodesia's Unilateral Declaration of Independence in 1965 was brought to an end and the independent state of Zimbabwe created. The CMF was responsible for monitoring the implementation of the cease-fire agreement between the Rhodesian regime's forces and the guerrillas of the Patriotic Front, during the period leading up to independence. It had a strength of 1,397 drawn mainly from the United Kingdom, but including smaller contingents from three other Commonwealth countries. The New Zealand Army contributed 74 officers and men to this force.

Multinational Force and Observers (MFO)

The Multinational Force and Observers (MFO) was created in April 1982 on the initiative of the United States and opposed by the Soviet Union, the MFO was designed to supervise Israel's withdrawal from the Sinai following the Camp David Accords of September 1978 and the Egypt-Israel Peace Treaty of March 1979. The MFO numbers approximately 2,600 of whom about half are American. Since 1986 the New Zealand Army has contributed to the MFO every six months two engineers, eight drivers a 12 man New Zealand Army training and advisory team. In 1989 a New Zealand officer, Lieutenant General D. S. McIver took command of the MFO.

The New Zealand Army — A Worldwide Contribution

The New Zealand Army under the auspices of such organisations such as the Mutual Aid Programme, the United Nations, and the Ministry of External Relations and Trade/Government direction, regularly sends soliders on operations, exercises, projects or courses to: Antarctica (New Zealand Support Unit/New Zealand Army Cargo Detachment), England, Norway, Cook Islands, Papua New Guinea, Moscow, Saudi Arabia, Singapore, Malaysia, Canada, Pakistan, Syria, Israel, Egypt, USA, Tonga, Belize, Hong Kong, Indonesia, Germany, Brunei, Vanuatu, Australia, Solomons, Kermedec Islands, and the Tokelaus.

Apart from this the New Zealand Army regularly aids the Civilian community with Civil Defence, (flood damage, earthquake damage, disasters, etc), the New Zealand Police (search and rescue, missing people, bomb disposal) as well as aiding community groups such as the Scouts. A significant level of support was provided by the Army to the 1990 Celebrations, the Royal Visit, the Commonwealth Games and the Waitangi Day celebrations.

New Zealand Contribution to the Multinational Forces in the Gulf

In 1990, the New Zealand Government made the decision to commit a contingent of Army medical personnel to the Gulf theatre.

On 16 January, 32 personnel forming the 1st New Zealand Army Medical Team left for the Gulf. The team, a group of highly skilled professionals consisting of surgeons, theatre nurses, and medical assistants, left with the support and best wishes of the Government and the vast majority of New Zealanders, to work with a 500 bed deployable United States fleet hospital in Manaha, Bahrain.

The New Zealand Defence Force Medical Team, this time consisting of five Army personnel in a tri-service contingent of 20, left on the 27th January, 1991 to be attached to a British fixed-base hospital in Muharraq, Bahrain. The Army team included a medical officer, an environmental health officer, a medical clerk, a dental officer and a dental assistant.

Queen Elizabeth II, Army Memorial Museum, Waiouru

On October 15, 1978, the Queen Elizabeth II Army Memorial Museum was formally opened by Sir Keith Holyoake. The museum serves as a memorial to all those who have served in the New Zealand Army in peace and war. Location: Adjacent to State Highway One at the Southern entrance to Waiouru and is open between 9am-4.30pm everyday except Christmas. Phone 0658-56-234.

The Army Career

A peacetime Army requires highly trained personnel in most skills and vocations to enable mobilisation during times of need to occur smoothly, with the ability to train and support large numbers of personnel in short periods of time.

Personnel may enter as either: Regular Force adults, Regular force Cadets, Regular Force Officers, Territorial Force Officers or soldiers.

For further information on these categories please contact your nearest recruiter under Armed Forces Recruiting in the phone book or Free Phone 0800 732-666.

CONCLUSION

After a century and a half of development the personnel of the New Zealand Army are the inheritors of an enviable tradition; valiant duty faithfully done. It is a tradition that all New Zealanders share and indeed it is one of the binding traditions of our society.

While it is impossible to predict the future for the Army, it can be stated that it will change. Indeed, one of the constants of its history is continual change. Another constant appears to be the forgetfulness of the nation. In time of crisis support is over–whelming, in time of peace it is grudgingly given. As the nature of the world has tended to be the lurch from crisis to crisis, it would have perhaps made more sense to have constant rather than fluctuating support for the nation's ground forces.

If the country is to guarantee its own defence in an insecure world, then it will have to support national security in the same way it provides for social security. Without a secure sovereign state there tends to be no other securities for a nation's citizens.

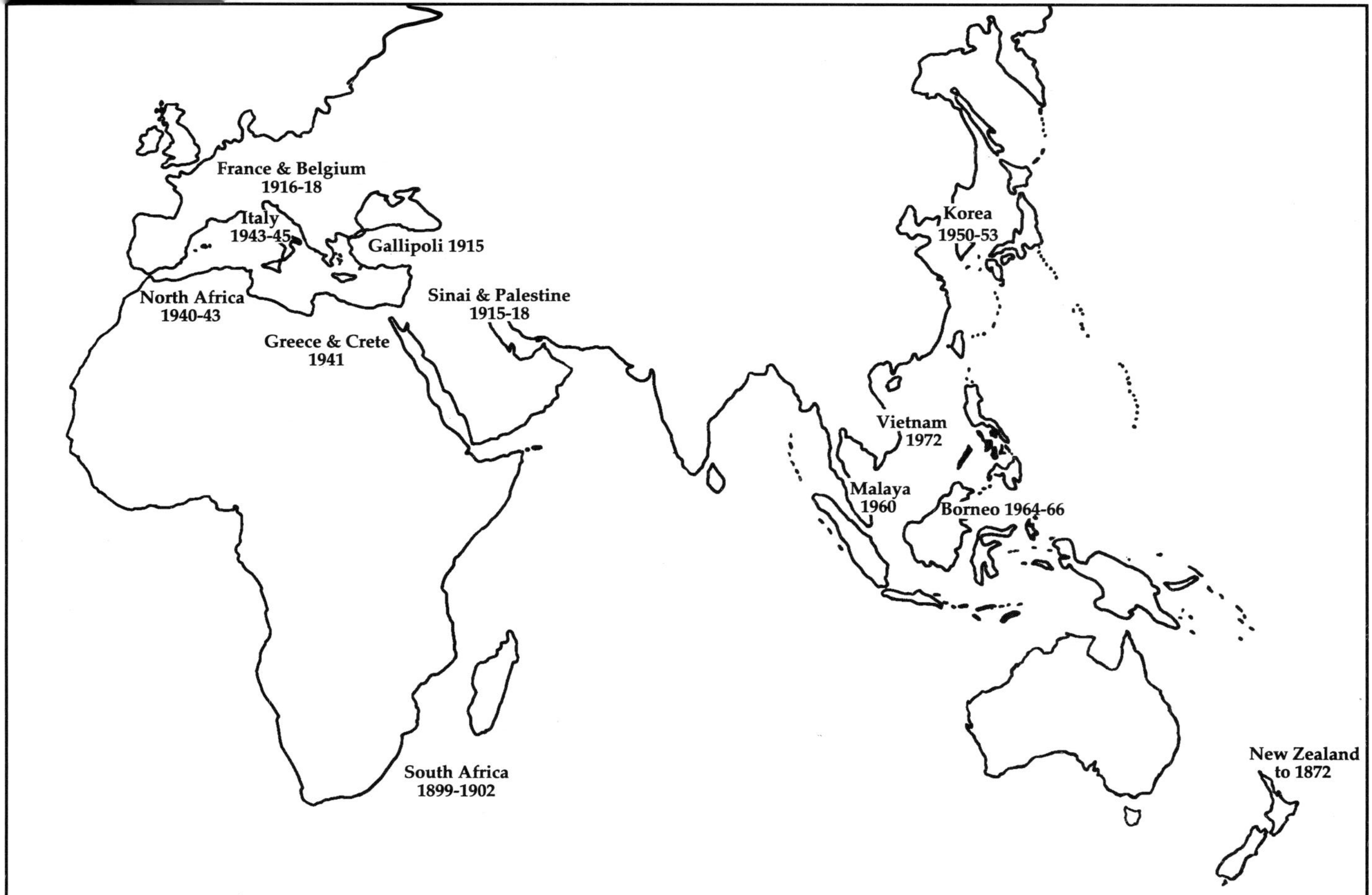

Major theatres of combat for New Zealand Troops

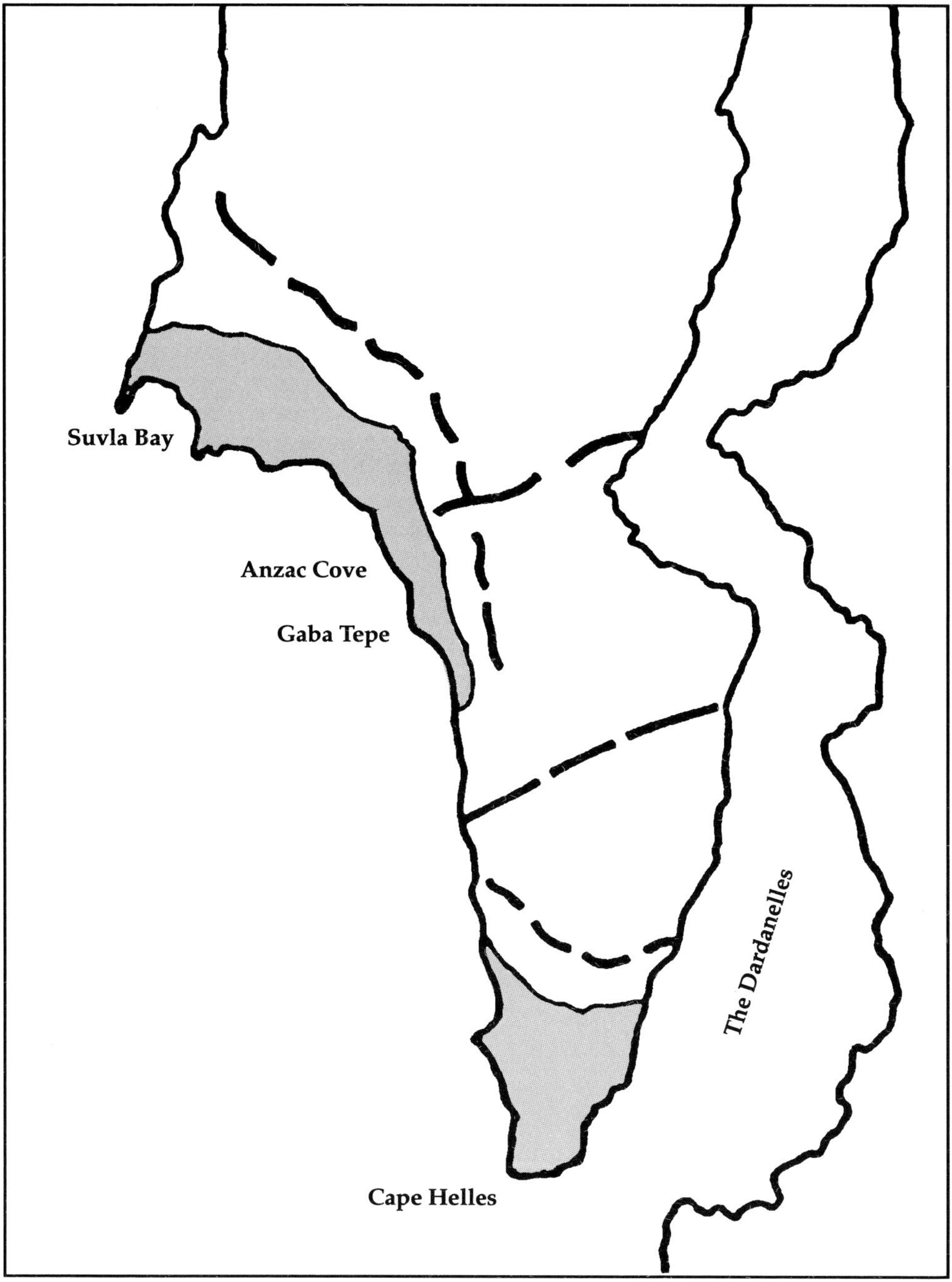

Gallipoli Peninsula 1915.
(shaded areas show allied footholds)

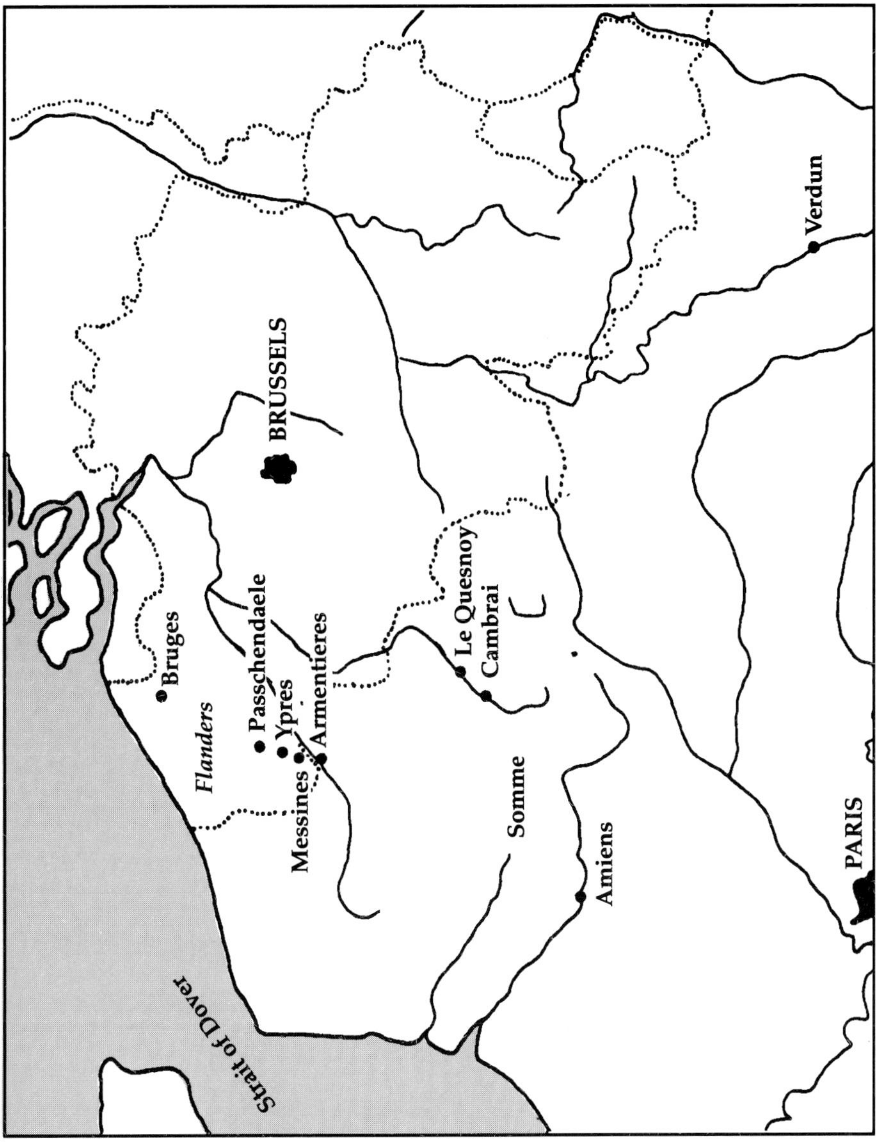

The Western Front 1916-1918.

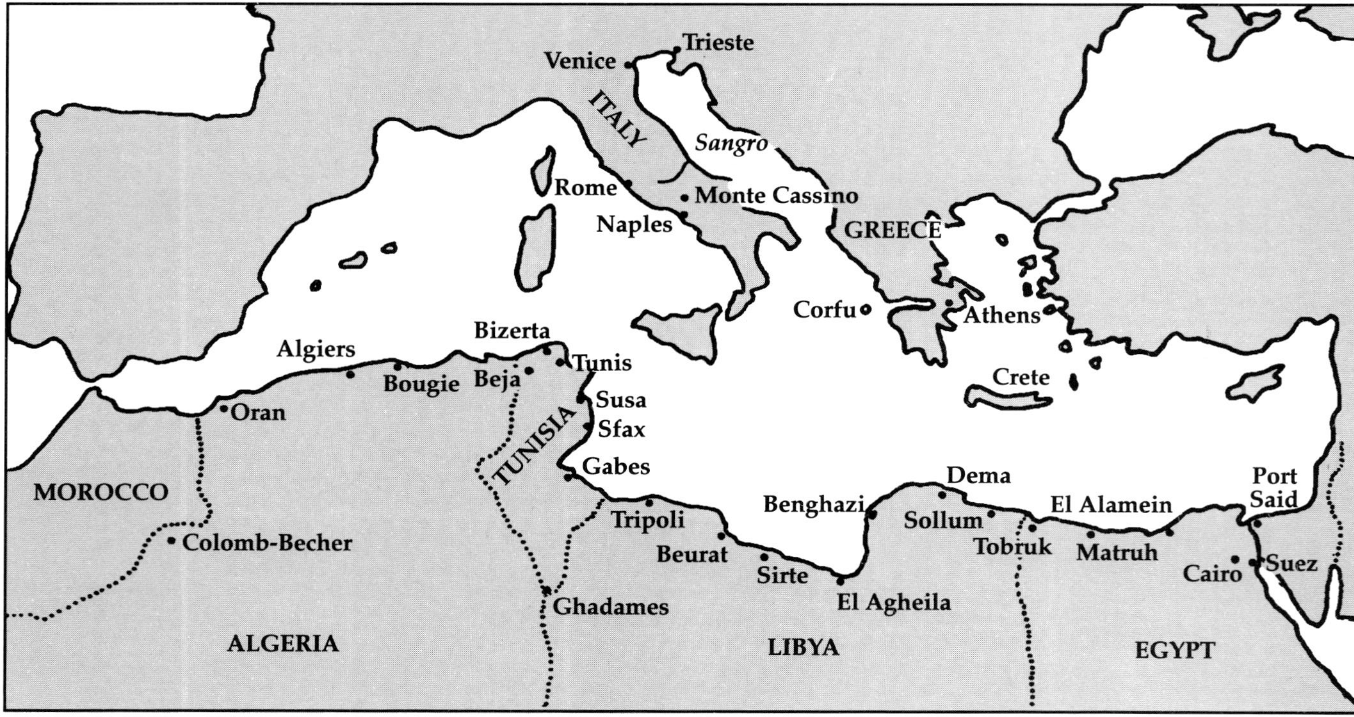

North African and Mediterranean theatres of war 1941-1945.

CHRONOLOGY

1827-Jan:	A detachment of the 57th Regiment drilled by prisoners at Kororareka.
1834-Sep:	Expedition of 50th Regiment and Royal Marines rescue Guard Family in Taranaki.
1840-Feb:	Signing of the Treaty of Waitangi.
1843-Jun:	Wairau "Massacre".
1844-Jul:	Sacking of Kororareka by Hone Heke.
1845-Mar:	Attack on Kororareka.
	Passing of first Militia Ordinance.
May:	Unsuccessful British attack on Puketutu Pa.
Jun:	Unsuccessful British attack on Ohaeawai Pa.
1846-Jan:	Successful attack on Ruapekapeka Pa.
1858-Jun:	Passing of the Militia Act.
1860-Apr:	Start of Taranaki and Waikato Anglo-Maori Wars.
1863-May:	Colonial Defence Act 1862 comes into effect.
Aug:	Raising of Taranaki Bush Rangers.
1864-Apr:	Battle of Gate Pa.
1867-Oct:	Disbandment of Special Forces. Passing of Armed Constabulary Act.
1870-Feb:	Last British regiment (the 18th) leaves New Zealand.
1872-Feb:	Official end of Anglo-Maori Wars.
1878	First "Russian Scare".
1886-Sep:	Armed Constabulary divided into the Police and Field Force.
1899-Sep:	New Zealand offers contingent for Anglo-Boer War.
1900-Feb:	Relief of Kimberley.
1902-May:	Boers surrender.
1909-Feb:	Passing of the Defence Act.
1914-Aug:	War declared against Germany.
	German Samoa occupied.
Dec:	Main Body arrives in Egypt.
1915-Feb:	First combat action on the Suez Canal.
Apr:	Landing on Gallipoli peninsula.
Aug:	Battle for Chunuk Bair.
Dec:	Withdrawal from Anzac Cove.
1916-Apr:	NZ Mounted Rifle Brigade deployed to Sinai peninsula.
	NZ Division arrives in France.
Sep:	The Somme.
1917-Mar:	First Battle of Gaza.
Apr:	Second Battle of Gaza.
Jun:	Messines.
Jul-Nov:	Ypres
Sep:	Polygon Wood.
Oct:	Passchendaele.
	Capture of Beersheba
Nov:	Occupation of Jaffa.
1918-Mar:	German advance on Western Front.

Feb:	Capture of Jericho.
Mar:	Battle of Amman.
Jul:	Allied advance on Western Front.
Sep:	Surrender of Turkish Army.
Oct:	Le Cateau and Selle River.
Nov:	Le Quesnoy and surrender of German Armies.
1921-Aug:	Official end of World War I.
Dec:	Disbandment of NZEF.
1931-Jun:	Suspension of compulsory clause of the 1909 Defence Act.
1937-Jul:	Council of Defence formed.
1939-Sep:	War declared on Germany. Raising of 6600-strong all-volunteer "Special Force".
Oct::	Raising of 28 (Maori) Battalion.
Dec:	"2nd NZ Expeditionary Force" adopted as official title.
1940 -	Deployment of 2nd NZ Division to Egypt and the U.K.
Nov:	8 Brigade established in Suva, Fiji.
Dec:	First Libyan Campaign.
1941-Apr:	Battle for Greece.
May:	Battle of Crete.
Nov:	2nd NZ Division in Egypt is together for the first time as a complete entity (nearly 20,000 men).
Dec:	War declared on Japan.
1942-Jan:	14 Brigade established in Fiji and B-Force assumes divisional status.
Feb:	2nd NZ Division deploys to Syria.
May:	"3rd NZ Division" title adopted by B-Force.
Jun:	2nd NZ Division returns from Syria for the start of the five-month Battle for Egypt. 2nd NZ Division withdraws from Minquar Qaim.
Jul:	Rout of the Italian "Ariete Division". Battles for Ruweisat Ridge and El Mreir Depression
Sep:	Battle of Alam el Halfa.
Oct:	N and T-Forces deploy to Norfolk Island and Tonga. Battle of El Alamein. Advance Party of 3rd NZ Division deploys to New Caledonia.
Nov:	Pursuit starts of retreating Axis forces from Alamein Line.
Dec:	2nd NZ Division executes the "left hook" around Axis forces at El Agheila.
1943-Jan:	Capture of Tripoli.
Mar:	The NZ Corps (2nd NZ Division, 8th Armoured Brigade and L-Force (Free French) outflank the Mareth Line breaking through the Axis forces at the Tebaga Gap.
Apr:	Battle for Takrouna.
May:	Axis Forces in Tunisia surrender. 2nd NZ Division returns 1900 miles to Egypt.

Aug:	3rd NZ Division arrives in Guadalcanal.
Sep:	Italian armistice signed.
	Landing on Vella Lavella.
	NZ Squadron of the Long Range Desert Group deploys to the Aegean Islands.
Oct:	2nd NZ Division sails from Egypt bound for Italy.
	Vella Lavella declared secure.
	Italy declares war on Germany.
	Landing on Mono and Stirling Islands in the Treasury Islands.
	Organised Japanese resistance ceases in Treasury Islands.
	2nd NZ Division occupies a sector of 8th Army front near the Adriatic coast and crosses the Sangro River.
Dec:	N-Force withdrawn from Norfolk Island.
	Orsogna captured after three weeks of fighting.
	NZ Squadron of Long Range Desert group disbanded.
1944-Feb:	Start of Battle of Cassino for the New Zealanders.
	Landing on Nissan Island.
Apr:	2nd NZ Division withdrawn from Cassino battle.
Jul:	Last New Zealand troops withdrawn from the Solomons.
	2nd NZ Division advances towards Florence.
Sep:	2nd NZ Division deployed to eastern Italian front.
Oct:	3rd NZ Division disbanded in New Zealand.
1945-Apr:	Crossing of the Senio River.
May:	Trieste occupied.
	Germany surrenders.
Aug:	Japan surrenders.
Oct:	J-Force formed in Italy.
1946-Jan:	HQ 2nd NZ Division disbanded in Italy.
Mar:	J-Force arrives in Kure.
1948-Oct:	J-Force returns to New Zealand.
1949-Aug:	National referendum on conscription held.
1950-May:	First Intake of CMT.
Jun:	South Korea invaded by the North Koreans.
Jul:	NZ Army commitment to UN Force in Korea announced.
Dec:	Kayforce arrives in Pusan, Korea.
1951-Apr:	Battle of Kaypong.
1953-Jun:	Ceasefire announced in Korea.
1954-Jul:	Korean armistice signed.
1955-Jun:	1st NZSAS Squadron raised at Waiouru.
Dec:	1st NZSAS Squadron deploys to Malaya for the Emergency.
1957-Aug:	Last elements of Kayforce return to New Zealand.
Dec:	1st Battalion, The NZ Regiment deploys to Malaya.
	End of CMT announced.
1959-Nov:	2nd Battalion, The NZ Regiment deploys to Malaya.
1960-Jul:	The end of the Malayan Emergency.
1962-May:	First Intake of National Emergency.

1964-Jun:	RNZE detachment deployed to South Vietnam.
Aug:	Start of Confrontation between Malaysia and Indonesia.
1965-May:	NZ Government announces combat assistance to SouthVietnam.
Jul:	161 Battery deployed to Bien Hoa.
1966-Jun:	161 Battery redeployed in Nui Dat under command of HQ 1st Australian Task Force.
Aug:	End of Confrontation.
1967-May:	Victor One rifle company deployed to Nui Dat. NZ Services Medical Team deployed to Bong Son.
Dec:	Whisky One rifle company deployed to Nui Dat.
1968-Nov:	NZSAS troop deployed to Nui Dat.
1970-Oct:	1st NZ Army Training Team deployed to Chi Lang.
1971-Dec:	Withdrawal of last combat elements from South Vietnam.
1972-Feb:	2nd NZ Army Training Team deployed to Dong Ba Thin.
Apr:	Defence Act 1971 comes into force.
Dec:	Withdrawal of all NZ Army elements from SouthVietnam. End of National training announced.
1978-Oct:	Queen Elizabeth II Army Memorial Museum opened.
1979-Apr:	NZ Army Truce Monitoring Contingent deployed to Rhodesia.
1980-Mar:	NZATMC returns to New Zealand.
1982-Apr:	New Zealand Army personnel arrive in the Sinai as part of the Multi-National Force and observers (MFO)
1984-Jan:	Army restructured around a 1,200 man Regular Force Ready Reaction Force with an Integrated Expansion Force containing both Regular and Territorial Force soldiers in a brigade group. Both the RRF and IEF are supported by a Force Màintenance Group.
1985-Jan:	Officer Cadet School of New Zealand established at Waiouru, taking over functions previously carried out by the Officer Cadet Training Unit and the Officer Cadet Training Company.
1986-Apr:	Six women soldiers made the first female military parachute descent in New Zealand into the Waitemata Harbour.
Jul:	Defence and Security: what New Zealanders want (Corner Report) published in
1989-Nov:	Ministry of Defence restructured into two divisions, a policy Ministry of Defence and anoperational New Zealand Defence Force.
Dec:	New Zealand Defence: Resource Management Review (Quigley Report) published.
1990-Apr:	Legislation passed to formalise Ministry of Defence restructure.
Dec:	NZ Government announces Medical assistance to Gulf.